BORN IN 1949?
WHAT ELSE HAPPENED?

RON WILLIAMS

AUSTRALIAN SOCIAL HISTORY

BOOK 11 IN A SERIES OF 35
FROM 1939 to 1973

War Babies Years (1939 to 1945): 7 Titles
Baby Boom Years (1946 to 1960): 15 Titles
Post Boom Years (1961 to 1973): 13 Titles

BOOM, BOOM BABY, BOOM

Born in 1949? What else happened?

Published by Boom Books

Wickham, NSW, Australia

Web: www.boombooks.biz

© Ron Williams 2012. Fifth printing 2023

Creator: Williams, Ron, 1934- author
Title: Born in 1949? : what else happened? / Ron Williams.
ISBN: 9780648324430
Series: Born in series, book 11.
Australia--History--Miscellanea--20th century.

Cover images: National Archives of Australia.

 A1200, L58949, Arthur Calwell;

J2364, 2594/15, Flying Doctor dentist;

A1200, L12203, lawn bowls;

M1483/23/4, Family portrait.

TABLE OF CONTENTS

IMPORTANT PEOPLE AND EVENTS

King of England	George VI
Prime Minister of Australia	Ben Chifley
Leader of Opposition	Bob Menzies
Governor General	William McKell
Pope	Pius XII
PM of England	Clement Atlee
President of America	Harry Truman
Emperor of Japan	Hirohito

WINNER OF THE ASHES

1946 - 1947	Australia 3 - 0
1948	Australia 4 - 0
1950 - 1951	Australia 4 - 1

MELBOURNE CUP WINNERS

1948	Rimfire
1949	Foxzami
1950	Comic Court

ACADEMY AWARDS

Best Actor	Laurence Olivier
Best Actress	Jane Wyman

PREFACE TO THIS SERIES: 1939 TO 1973

This book is the 11th in a series of Titles that I have researched and written. It tells a story about a number of important or newsworthy Australia-centric events that happened in 1949. The series covers each of the years from 1939 to 1973, for a total of 35 Titles.

I developed my interest in writing these books a few years ago at a time when my children entered their teens. My own teens started in 1947, and I tried to remember what had happened to me then. I thought of the big events first, like Saturday afternoon at the pictures, and cricket in the back yard, and the wonderful fun of going to Maitland on the train for school each day. Then I recalled some of the not-so-good things. I was an altar boy, and that meant three or four Masses a week. I might have thought I loved God at that stage, but I really hated his Masses. And the schoolboy bullies, like Greg Favel and the hapless Freddie Bevin. Yet, to compensate for these, there was always the beautiful, black headed, blue-sailor-suited June Brown, who I was allowed to worship from a distance.

I also thought about my parents. Most of the major events that I lived through came to mind readily. But after that, I realised that I really knew very little about these parents of mine. They had been born about the start of the Twentieth Century, and they died in 1970 and 1980. For their last 20 years, I was old enough to speak with a bit of sense. I could have talked to them a lot about their lives. I could have found out about the times they lived in. But I did not. I know almost nothing about them really. Their courtship? Working in the pits? The Lock-out in the Depression?

Losing their second child? Being dusted as a miner? The shootings at Rothbury? My uncles killed in the War? There were hundreds, thousands of questions that I would now like to ask them. But, alas, I can't. It's too late.

Thus, prompted by my guilt, I resolved to write these books. They describe happenings that affected people, real people. In 1949, there is some coverage of international affairs, but a lot more on social events within Australia. This book, and the whole series is, to coin a modern phrase, designed to push the reader's buttons, to make you remember and wonder at things forgotten. The books might just let nostalgia see the light of day, so that oldies and youngies will talk about the past and re-discover a heritage otherwise forgotten. Hopefully, they will spark discussions between generations, and foster the asking and the answering of questions that should not remain unanswered.

The sources of my material. I was born in 1934, so that I can remember well a great deal of what went on around me from 1939 onwards. But of course, the bulk of this book's material came from research. That meant that I spent many hours in front of a computer reading electronic versions of newspapers, magazines, Hansard, Ministers' Press releases and the like. My task was to sift out, day-by-day, those stories and events that would be of interest to the most readers. Then I supplemented these with materials from books, broadcasts, memoirs, biographies, government reports and statistics. And I talked to old-timers, one-on-one, and in organised groups, and to Baby Boomers about their recollections. People with stories to tell came out of the woodwork, and talked no end about the tragic, and funny, and commonplace events that have shaped their families and lives.

The presentation of each book. For each year covered, the end result is a collection of short Chapters on many of the topics that concerned ordinary people in that year.

I think I have covered most of the major issues that people then were interested in. On the other hand, in some cases I have dwelt a little on minor frivolous matters, perhaps to the detriment of more sober considerations. Still, in the long run, this makes the book more readable, and hopefully it will convey adequately the spirit of the times.

Each of the books is mainly Sydney based, but I have been **deliberately national in outlook**, so that readers elsewhere will feel comfortable that I am talking about matters that affected them personally. After all, housing shortages and strikes and juvenile delinquency involved **all** Australians, and other issues, such as problems overseas, had no State component in them. I expect I can make you wonder, remember, rage and giggle equally, no matter whence you hail.

INTRODUCTION TO 1949

A few carry-over situations from 1948 are worthy of mention.

When war came to the Pacific in the years from 1942 to 1945, the Australian Government quite sensibly said that most of the nation's resources must go to the so-called War Effort. Among other things, this meant that ordinary people would have to give up some of their way of life and submit to the rationing of many goods. So, food was rationed, and petrol and butter, and meat, and clothing, and the list could go on. And other goods were hard to get. Such as bike tyres, cement, newspapers, caraway seeds, ice chests, toothpaste, and whisky.

When the War was over, every one **hoped that this rationing would be lifted immediately. Alas, this was not the case.** Prime Minister Chifley argued that, because we imported so much stuff from overseas, we would spend too many of our precious US dollars if we bought up big on the rationed goods. So, he kept the screws on, and so screws remained on the rationed list.

At the end on 1948, however, 50,000 different items were removed from this list. **50,000!** That is a lot of items that had been on the restricted list. And, it was officially said, a second release of a similar size would come soon. What a relief, we all said.

Of course, many of these items had to come from overseas. So they had to be ordered, and shipped, and then distributed across this wide brown land. This meant that it might be months before some of them became generally available. Still, it looked like happy days would soon be here again.

One side effect of these releases was the impact it had on the Black Market. Since 1942, forbidden or rationed goods magically could be bought from unofficial sources if you had enough money. Somehow supplies were found and distributed to the highest bidders, in major breaches of all laws. A lot of them came from the military, especially American bases, and many of them came from old-fashioned smugglers. In any case, there was a flourishing

Black Market that had not been set-back at all by the ending of the War.

Now, however, with the dropping of the restrictions, the writing was on the wall, and the millionaire spivs controlling the Markets no doubt returned to making an honest living.

One big gripe remained, however. Petrol rationing was not ended. Our need for the US Dollar stopped the Government from offering this boon to our motorists, despite the fact that petrol was flowing freely in countries like England and New Zealand. Chifley maintained this policy until the next Federal election, a decision that many observers are certain cost him victory there.

At the same time, jobs were plentiful. There were a few complications, though. When the ex-Servicemen came back from their military duties, **some of them expected to get their old jobs back. In fact, the Government had promised them that.** But in practice, this was hard to police. For example, it was often argued by the current occupant that the job had changed, and so the old job was not there any more. There were a spate of administrative and legal battles fought over these matters.

Also, on the labour front, some women were displaced by servicemen returning home, and this caused some angst. Then too, there were faint murmurings about equal pay for women if they did the same job as men did. But, generally, it was thought **at the time** that a man supporting a wife and three children should get more pay than a young girl doing the same job. So females had to wait longer for times to change before they could get equal pay. But, apart from such hiccups, there were plenty of jobs to go round, so any able-bodied person could find work.

Of greater concern was the housing market. Since 1940, the building of residential housing had almost stopped. As the young lions returned home, found a mate, and started siring cubs, they needed dens to dwell in. They could live with Mum and Dad for a year or two, but now with money in their pockets, they were anxious to move into the suburban jungle.

So, they needed to borrow from a bank, and this meant dressing up in their finest regalia, keeping an appointment with the local bank manager, begging and crawling to His Lordship for a loan, and being refused on at least the first two occasions. I have covered this process in a few other Titles in this series, so I will just say **here** that it was harrowing and frustrating, and there were just **a few** Mickey Mouse alternatives. So that adequate housing was not available, and indeed this remained the case for another decade.

The Christian religion was dominant throughout the nation. During the War, attendances at churches increased, and the uttering of prays to God multiplied enormously. Now, however, a decline in both of these measures occurred, and the secularisation of the population seemed to be hastening. One of the common complaints was that Sunday sermons were pointless, and that in a world that was full of conflicts and doubts, pulpit advice was nowhere to be heard. Given that advances in all-consuming science were apparently challenging all the tenets of religion, this emerging decline in traditional forms of worship was set to continue for decades and more.

RADIO RULES THE WAVES

TV had not yet arrived in Australia, so that up-to-the minute news came via radio sets. These were stuck in a corner of kitchens all round the nation, they were big enough to be seen as items of furniture, they had outside wooden aerials that towered over every dwelling, and they supported an army of Government inspectors who patrolled non-stop checking that householders had wireless licences.

Most commercial stations had no **news services** of their own, so listeners got their news from the ABC, at 7 o' clock at night and about eight in the morning. This was given by an austere announcer, always with a slightly formal British accent, who started with a stiff "Here is the News from the ABC."

Before that each week night there were **the great Australian shows**. *Dad and Dave* told the on-going story of life in a farming village. *Martin's Corner* was about as deep, and told us all about life in a shop in a smallish suburb. Real depth, however, could be found in *Yes What* where students Greenbottle, Bottomley and Stanford sat at the feet of the masterly Dr Percy Pym.

About this time, weekly shows from Bob Dyer and Jack Davy stole the limelight. Dyer's *Pick a Box* drew massive audiences. So too did the weekday drama about life in the country with a show entitled *Blue Hills*. This show went on until late in the Seventies.

Sport was very popular. Test cricket was covered ball by ball, even when the game was played in Britain. All major footy matches were covered weekly and, with the horse races, dominated Saturday radio. Special events, like the Davis Cup, played over the Christmas break, had millions of Aussies listening breathlessly to the description of every serve and rally.

Commercial stations too enriched our culture, especially with their ad breaks. Little ditties such as those for *Sydney Flour* and *Aeroplane Jelly* will still be remembered by many. Pop music was the main fare for these stations and crooners Bing Crosby, Frank Sinatra, and new-boy Perry Como were in demand. US bands such as Tommy Dorsey and Glen Miller, and the Andrew Sisters, got a good run. The ABC frowned a little on this frivolity, and played hours and hours of classical music day and night.

Comment. Looking back, I can see that radio dominated households just as much as TV and Netflix does today. In radio days, people at night gathered round the set and listened. No one spoke, except during the ads, and any worthwhile story had its followers who talked about its characters to their workmates and neighbours. Very serious adults warned about the dangers to society from the addiction to radio, and occasionally Church Ministers railed against it from the pulpit as it interfered with the family praying together.

Then, there was **the strict censorship**. No swearing or naughty slang was permitted. A few years later, when Prince Phillip was at an Outback cattle station, he talked about the "bloody" cattle. This was picked up on audio and played on radio. The world fell in and the item was removed within minutes and the ABC apologised for weeks on radio and in the Press.

No mention of sex as a topic was countenanced, and even the **word** "sex" was banned.

I rate the after-dinner shows of 1949 as vastly entertaining. If I compare them with those on TV today, I think they were better, on the average. Granted, the **occasional** TV show is better, with all the advantages of visual presentation. But if you gave me the choice, a random night of modern TV-watching versus a random night of 1949-radio listening, I would go for the latter.

Maybe though, it just my nostalgia for the happy and care-free days of my youth that I am looking at. I suppose I will never find out.

LUXURY ON WATER

When the War in Europe started a decade ago, shipping round the world was taken over by Governments. Big boats and ships were confiscated so that troops and munitions and foodstuffs could be moved quickly from here to there at will. This meant that passenger liners were no longer available to sail holiday-makers on their traditional cruises from Australia to London. Instead, these ships were converted to troop carriers, and 6 weeks of luxury at sea were no longer on the agenda.

But now, at the start of 1949, a brand-new liner, the *Orcades*, was back on the route. This signaled that the six other Orient Line ships would soon be back on the High Seas, and the days of *Ship Ahoy* had returned.

MY RULES IN WRITING

Now we are just about ready to go. First, though, I give you a few Rules I follow as I write. They will help you understand where I am coming from.

Note. Throughout this book, I rely a lot on reproducing **Letters from the newspapers**. Whenever I do this, I put the text in a different font, and indent it a little, and make the font somewhat smaller. **I do not edit the text at all. The same is true for the *News Items* at the start of each Chapter.** That is, I do not correct spelling or if the text gets at all garbled, I do not correct it. It's just as it was seen in the Papers.

Second Note. The **material** for this book, when it comes from newspapers, is reported as it was seen at the time. If the benefit of hindsight over the years changes things, then I might record that in my Comments. **The info reported thus reflects matters as they were seen in 1949.**

Third Note. Let me also apologise in advance to anyone I might offend. In a work such as this, it is certain some people will think **I got some things wrong. I am sure that I did**, but please remember, all of this is only my opinion. And really, **my opinion does not matter one little bit in the scheme of things. I hope you will say "silly old bugger", and shrug your shoulders, and read on.**

OFF WE GO

So now we are ready to plunge into 1949. Let's go, and I trust you will have a pleasant trip.

JANUARY NEWS ITEMS

The New Year started with the news that **Don Bradman, probably the greatest human ever to be born**, had been knighted in the Queen's New Year's Honours list, for services to Cricket. **All Australians worth their salt stuck out their chests**, and bathed in the glory that we all rightly shared.

The headline from the *Sydney Morning Herald* gave **alarming news of an Emergency in Brisbane**. It reported that **a strike by garbage and night-soil workers** had been going on for two weeks, and that there was a danger of disease. Many residents were burying the offensive material....

The night-soil problem was particularly serious because **60 per cent of Brisbane was unsewered. Workers were striking** for more pay, better working conditions, and transport both to and from work....

These demands were echoed right throughout the nation in **strikes that were occurring all day every day**. It was often said that we were a "strike-bound nation"....

The above news report is also a reminder that, even in our capital cities, there were **many suburbs that lived with dunnies in their back yards**, with a weekly service that emptied them.

Society is changing. Divorces were becoming more common. Rates from all over the western world indicate that, compared to pre-War numbers, divorces were increasing at least five-fold....

At the same time, legal actions for **breach of promise** were showing a **steep decline**.

Six aboriginal Northern Territory stockmen were sheltering in the lee of a cliff during a storm. Lightning struck, and all received burns to their arms and legs at least. **Their leather belts also burned, and large holes were burnt into the soles of their leather shoes.** Three of the more serious cases were flown to hospital.

Victor Kravchenko is a **Russian** diplomat who has now written a book that talks about **the supposed evils of the Communist state.** A Paris newspaper gave it a very bad review and said that he was a drunkard and had faked the whole thing. He is suing the paper....

He is attracting **world-wide attention** in a **new era when the cold-War was hotting up**. **Soon** the world would be full of spies and bugging devices, anti-Red Senators in the USA, Commo influence in our Trade Unions, and defecting diplomats from England to Russia....

This was the beginning of an **almost hysterical period of 40 years** where most of the world divided into two camps, following either Russia or the USA....

If you **do** like this type of thing, you will be happy for the next 40 years. If you **don't**, then stay away from all forms of media for the period. It did not slow down until the Berlin Wall fell...

Thirty years later, it is back again. Four generations of Americans (and probably Russians too) have grown up with paranoia about Russia. **Can they ever change?**

TAKING IT EASY

New Year's Day got off to a quiet start in Sydney. In those days, there were no fireworks on the harbour or anywhere else, and the big adventure was to grab your girlfriend and head for King's Cross. There you could get drunk if you wanted to, perhaps get a hug or a kiss at midnight, and then find your way home without the aid of public transport. My recollection of these festivities is that no sensible person ever went twice. Still, in 1949, the papers reported that "thousands of people" assembled there, and "revelled".

But the Editorial-pages **in that year** were strangely restrained. Normally, they were full of messages from the King, and the Prime Minister, and the GG, and so on. This year they were missing. The revelry photos in the Herald normally ran to three pages over a few days, but this year there was only a single picture.

The *Sydney Morning Herald* (*SMH*) was able to fill its January pages with heaps of trivia. The Knighting of Don Bradman filled many column-inches with lots of photos. Then it kept its readers rapt with details of how many surfers had spent the previous day at Bondi Beach, and with reports of the distress of Council workers because the papers from the fish and chips were left in the gutter. (There was no suggestion that the right place for them was in a bin, because there were no bins in place in those days.)

There was also a riveting story that said that William Dobell had been awarded the Archibald Prize for his now-famous painting of Margaret Olley. And to add to the excitement, it was announced that a US film star, Rita Hayworth, was in big trouble at home because she was having a "flagrant" affair with a Pakistani Prince called Aly Khan. He was reportedly a fabulously rich man, who was married with a few children.

Many American mothers were aghast at the brazenness of the couple. Their Save-Our-Daughters Committees were busy contacting anyone who would listen, demanding that Hayworth's films be withdrawn from circulation, and that Aly's horses should not be allowed to enter in horse-racing events world-wide.

In Melbourne, a Presbyterian spokesman said he supported a ban on viewing her films, and wanted the film industry to proceed towards higher standards of conduct. He was supported by Baptist Rev Jarvis, who expressed "abhorrence" at the whole business. "Anything that attacks the sanctity of marriage is completely against Christian principles and everything that is right and proper."

On the other hand, in Sydney, Rev Cowie, of Crown Street Memorial Church, said a boycott would serve no useful purpose because no one would take any notice of it. A "leading authority" of the Catholic Church added that the Church was **more interested in the actual films** screened than in the private lives of the actors. He thought that Miss Hayworth **could not be condemned unless half of Hollywood was condemned with her**.

KEEP YOUR EYES ON INDONESIA

One overseas-related event that caught attention in the period of summer torpor came from an editorial in the *SMH*. It all came about because **the Dutch, the white occupiers**

of Indonesia, were under attack from the native population who wanted them to go home. Violence was sporadic but constant and serious, and there was every sign that it would rise to the point where a bloody revolution would occur. India, for some reason, decided that it should hold a conference of the interested nations that lived on the fringes of Indonesia, and it **invited Australia to attend**. Needless to say, we were to be the only white nation represented there.

The Editor of the *SMH* came out with an editorial that would probably make the writer of it **now** curl up into a small ball. His attitude was that Australia was a white nation and that we **should not be mixing in with other Asian nations as if we had something in common with them**. He thought that the Asian nations should fix their own problems and that we in Australia were separate from them, and that we should be careful to make that clear.

If Asians wanted to get rid of the white man, that was their problem, but we as white men should have nothing to do with them. **"Why is white Australia expected to lend a hand?"** The editorial asked "Our Government has accepted the invitation to attend. **What infatuation is driving us to consort in an anti-European convention** with those to whom our white-Australia policy is anathema?"

The assumption that Australia is included in the Asian space is totally false, he said. "We are striving to maintain a white homogeneous population, **unmarked by any stain of colour**." It is obvious that India's Nehru is seeking to seduce Australia from the West, and that we are foolish to have accepted his invitation. In fact, **"it is the wildest folly to have played into his hands."**

This is as strong a statement of **the White Australia Policy** as you will get. **At the time, it was strongly supported, by most Australians.** There was the occasional voice raised against it, indeed enough to suggest that perhaps a change might come some time in the future. But that was a long way off.

One prominent Australian, however, did speak up against it. A well-known historian raised his voice. Charles Bean had been appointed Official Historian of Australian efforts in WWI, and had written several Volumes on the War. He was also respected as a person who made sound commentary on a wide range of social issues to the Press.

Letters, C Bean. Far from feeling that it is dangerous for us to confer with nations in the Asian sphere, **some of us apprehend an even greater danger** – namely the development of **a world separated into two sections by colour** .

A division leading to a third world war on the basis of colour, would be the crowning glory of human stupidity.

Our present divisions in all walks of life do not separate us from the East. They, too, draw their inspiration from the same philosophies of liberty and humanity that we do, and base on those principles their hopes for their peoples. Surely, every principle of sound statesmanship should urge us to act **as interpreters between East and**

West, and if we disagree, give each the benefit of our frank advice.

The White Australia Policy depends on strength, but strength based on the right of a people fit for nationhood in control of its own compositions; and it provides another reason why we **cannot afford to dissociate ourselves from those who are still Eastern members of the British Commonwealth**.

Supporters of the White Australia Policy **sprang to reply.**

Letters, D Watts. From all that has been said and done, it would seem that the proposed conference will contribute nothing to the resolving of the difficulties, but will in fact be an anti-white, pro-Indonesian assembly. As such, **it is more likely to lead us one stage further towards a world-wide conflict than to prevent it**.

Since the Dutch and Indonesians cannot come to an amicable agreement, it were better to try to isolate the affair, that it may remain a local disturbance, than to drag it into the world arena, as Indians and Australians seem bent on doing.

Without a doubt there are, as Dr Bean remarks, elements in Asia that draw inspiration from the same philosophies of liberty and humanity as we do, but on the other hand there are elements as greedy, cruel, and false as anywhere in the world. **Among semi-civilised or unsettled people, it is men of the latter type who, because of their ruthlessness, rise to power.**

There is nothing in the present state of affairs in Asia to assure us that such men will not eventually, where they have not already, become the directors of the Asian region. **Australians, however well-disposed towards Asians, would receive neither gratitude nor mercy from such men if they were to fall into their hands.**

Two Australian delegates did attend the convention, merely as observers. It should surprise no-one that the gathering left no mark in history, and that this little storm in Australia stayed well within its own teacup. But **later in the year**, as we will see, the Minister for Immigration, **Arthur Calwell, made a most controversial application of the White Australia Policy**, that stirred many a person to question, for the first time, just how proper it was that we should maintain it.

POMS AND DAGOS ARE HERE TO STAY

By the end of January, migration into Australia was flowing at a rapid rate. Many of the newcomers were British, and lots of these came here on fares as low as ten Pounds per person. This low price was made possible because the Government had accepted the idea that this nation needed to either **populate or perish**, and was thus keen to **get those reliable Brits to settle down here.**

But there were **also increasing numbers of "Poles and Balts"**, from sundry parts of Europe, and these people were often housed for years in camps that had previously been used as army bases during the War. This group faced great difficulties with the English language and the Australian culture, as well as finding work in a local workplace that was, at least, **suspicious of anyone with a foreign accent**.

I dare not at this stage forget to mention our friends from the Mediterranean region who also flocked in. Families from Greece went in ship-loads to Melbourne, and Italians went to suburbs like Sydney's Leichhardt, and Newcastle's Hamilton. **Strangely, the Italians, who had fought against us during the War, had little resentment directed towards them. In contrast, the Japanese were aggressively hated for decades by many living here.**

> **Personal note.** I was at High School when half a dozen Polish early-teenagers came to our school in Maitland. Maitland was never accused of being cosmopolitan, and indeed it turned out that it was far from that. **The whole school simply ignored these young lads. This was not a deliberate policy.** It was just that they were seen as adding nothing, and with the language problems, it was just easier to go on as if they were not there.
>
> These lads were sent all the way from Greta migrant camp every day so that they might get a Catholic education. But, as it proved, faith alone would not save them, and within a month, they had dwindled away, and gone back to the **local State schools, where they could be ignored without so much travel**.

MUSICA NON VIVA

Now that the War was well out of the way, many people were hoping that the major orchestras in the nation could start producing the fine symphonic music that was available before the War. At first glance, it seemed that they would be frustrated, because **the four major orchestras**, that had been performing before the War, **were struggling** to come back to life.

By now, in 1949, it seemed that **two of these would be resurrected**, and this gave great hope to classical music enthusiasts. Players were recruited, a few concerts had been given, and the whole music scene was agog with the hopes that these performances heralded for the future.

Of, course, there is always someone who spoils things. In the case, it was the Australian Musicians Union. This Union, like all other Unions, could refuse membership to persons that it picked out, and once that happened, those persons could not play music commercially in Australia.

In this case, it picked out all musicians from overseas. The only exception were Britishers, who **would be permitted to play after 10 years' residence in Australia**. The Union argued that an influx of overseas talent would take jobs from Australians, and it contended that this nation had a fine body of musicians who were just as capable as those from overseas.

Eugine Goossens, the Conductor of the Sydney Symphonic Orchestra, was the current Father of serious music in Australia. When he thundered, everyone listened. And in this case, he **did** thunder. First of all, he knocked the Poms in general. "Anyone living in England on 14 pennyworth of meat and two eggs a month" would be eager to come to Australia to work.

Then he came up with some facts. By international standards, there is a shortage of **first-class** Australian musicians locally. This curtails our programmes, and means that audiences can hear only the most hackneyed works. The teaching of music is so bad that it has produced a generation of players lacking style and the technical brilliance required. Many of the players cannot pass elementary sight-reading and aural tests at rehearsals. He went on to praise a few of our current players, and to actually **name** quite a few who were not, he said, up to standard.

The *SMH* fully agreed with Goossens. It published an editorial under the header "Another blow to our cultural heritage." It bemoaned that the Union move "underlined the small-mindedness, as well as the inevitable evil consequence, of this dog-in-the-manger Union decree."

It went on to say that Australian musicians were always **welcome in England**. And then to the wider argument that "such closed-shop practices were utterly alien to the practice of the Arts in general."

There was a lot of other support for Goossens.

Letters, Horace Green, State Conservatorium of Music. Orchestral playing has reached an amazingly high degree of proficiency nowadays, and experience has proved that symphony orchestras do not survive, or indeed, deserve to survive, in Australia or any other country unless this high standard is maintained.

In spite of the arguments put forward by Mr Kitson, which are, in the main, inaccurate, it is well known to all discerning musicians that certain of our orchestras will never attain anything like the standards attained by many European and American organisations unless some highly trained and experienced instrumentalists are recruited.

It is, therefore, the primary duty of the Musicians' Union to protect the welfare of both its present and future members by doing its utmost to promote and not hinder progress to this goal.

Another Letter-writer pointed out that if this nation banned overseas music professionals, then it could be expected that **other nations would in turn prohibit Australians**. He saw that as being a disaster, especially for the young, who often sought experience overseas.

There were, however, other writers who supported the Union move.

Letters, Australia First. In his article, Goossens says that he realises the ballet and opera orchestras will soon be disbanded, but that these 70 out-of-work musicians will not mind foreigners coming out here to take available work.

Who do you think you're kidding, Mr Goossens?

By inference, I take it that Mr Goossens would like to see a big pool of unemployed musicians, of high ranking, just hanging around waiting for a vacancy in the ABC. This would tend to knock any nonsense out of the players already working for the ABC.

One writer argued that two of Australia's major orchestras were, right now, closing down. That would mean that many people would be out of work. Could anyone say that these locals should not have preference over overseas applicants? At least for the next few years, until the glut of players had been worked out of the system?

Another writer suggested that the surplus musicians could **find employment in picture theatres**. This sounds strange now, but back in 1949 a few major city theatres employed orchestras on Saturday afternoons and nights and special occasions to comfort patrons while they were waiting for the programme to start. Supposedly, the music added a bit of class to the theatre.

But these orchestras were generally considered to be weak. They did provide work for up-and-comers who wanted the experience and money on the way to the top. But serious musicians, who had played with a major orchestra, would never lower themselves to play for Saturday afternoon movie-theatre crowds.

Goossens offered a half-way conciliatory suggestion that **perhaps a quota could be approved every year**. That would mean that about four talented musicians would be given entry each year.

Another worthy idea was put forward. It suggested that vacancies be advertised here and overseas, and the best applicants be offered jobs. They would come here at their own expence, and compete on the same basis as Australians. If they seemed to be the best, they would get the job, with no Union restraints on them.

Comment. There was no immediate solution to this matter. It really was a new version on an old, and on-going, theme.

The Union, quite rightly from its point of view, wanted to protect its members. Someone else in society wanted to change the status quo. In the long run, as the world changed, the inevitable happened and, in this case, the Union had to back down.

That is what happened in this case. Quickly, our displaced musicians found that they were in demand overseas, and many moved to most places in the world. While there, they gained employment, and doubtless lifted their standards, so that they could later return to Australia and then meet Goossens' high demands.

While this was happening, over the next decade, Australia started to welcome American entertainers in droves. People like Johnny Ray, Burl Ives, Frank Sinatra, Wayne Newton flooded in, and brought with them their own bands. They **were** required to join our Musicians Unions, but this was only token. Once here, they could do what they liked. In the face of this influx and outflow of foreigners, the Union finally backed off and relaxed their ban on the free movement of our musicians.

FEBRUARY NEWS ITEMS

Various Traffic authorities in NSW **will police taxis** in the State to ensure that **drivers do not allow their braces or underwear to be seen**. In future, they must also be clean-shaven and clean and tidy. Recommended apparel for summer is a **safari jacket** (remember them?), and for winter, **a collar and tie. "The War is over. There is now no excuse for slovenly appearance."**

Comment. The authorities could have spent their time better by commanding the tide not to come in.

The Prime Minister, Ben Chifley, has spent a few days **talking to officials from a US company called General Motors Holden.** It seems that, if they got certain guarantees of co-operation from Australia, they would set up facilities for us **to build cars in Australia**.

Comment. This seems unlikely to happen. Apart from our never-ending **trouble with our Unions**, it seems to many experts that **our market here is too small**.

Second comment. We all know that **Holden (and Ford) did set up here**. It took them 70 years to learn that **our market was indeed too small** and that our Unions would demand too much for long-term profitability.

When the Pacific War started, **taxation** on the average family **rose sharply, up about 50 per cent over two years.** Last December, the Government approved tax cuts of about 10 per cent. **Now it says it will make further cuts of 30 per cent.** Though they will not come into effect until next year....

Comment. No one looked this gift horse in the mouth, but it was often noted, and said, that 1949 was an election year, and maybe - just **maybe - this had influenced the Government** to loosen the purse strings....

But.... No, No. No Government would be so sly.

While the Oz Government was providing **some post-war relief**, the Catholic Church was going the opposite way. **In 1941**, the world was at war, so the Church said **it would no longer enforce restrictions on fasting and abstinence**. These rules said that at certain times, like Lent, Catholics could not eat meat at all, and had to cut down on their total food intake....

Now that the War is over, and people could get whatever food they wanted, **Church rules were to be imposed again**. So, for example, in Lent (a 40 day period) and every Friday, **meat will be off the menu, and gluttony and debauchery must be postponed for a while**.

A narrow escape: News from the Outback. The Guthrie family at a cattle station in South Australia **received a package** sent to them by air. When they opened it, **a large black snake** was coiled inside. They called the airline, who said it was not their business.

They sent urgent telegrams to the relatives who had sent the package. They had no knowledge of the snake. They took it to the local Police Station. A constable struck it three times with a black ebony ruler. It was clearly dead. They lifted it and found that **it was made from genuine rubber, perfectly moulded and showing every scale**.

BACK TO REALITY

This whole nation in 1949 took the month off between Christmas Day and Australia Day, and forgot about all the news that bedevils us for the rest of the year. Luckily, this tradition has persisted till the present day, and happily we can still re-charge our batteries at this time.

But now, forget the bliss of Summer. Gird your loins up for harsh reality. There is still a world out there, and it's our job to fix it.

CHINA SEES RED

The events in China could not be ignored. The Nationalists Government, led by Chiang Kai-Shek, had about 1934 started chasing the Communist Red Armies towards the West of the nation. This is the period of the fabled Long March. When World War II came, **the two Chinese Armies combined against the Japanese**, and both got a huge amount of military equipment from the US. After the War, they returned to their fighting, and used this equipment to slaughter each other.

By 1949, the Communists were in control of most of the nation, and were on the point of capturing the major cities on the East Coast. The cities of Nanking and Shanghai appeared about to fall, and it seemed that the Nationalists were about to formally surrender. Below is a typical news report from Nanking.

The Nationalist Government announced today that an army of 200,000 troops had been destroyed near Suchow today. Many of the remaining government officials in Nanking made hurried preparations to leave that city as the news came through.

This defeat represents one of the most ghastly stories in this most ghastly of wars. For days now, the encircling Communist forces have been firing American cannons at point blank range into a sea of human flesh crammed into an ever-diminishing small space. The Government troops were packed so tightly into trenches that every round of shell fire and every mortar was causing up to 15 casualties. Frozen, starving, defeated troops waded in the blood of their companions, and little was done for the wounded – not that anything much is ever done for Chinese wounded.

This Communist victory will leave 350,000 additional troops free to join with other attackers menacing Shanghai.

It should be pointed out that the war between the Reds and the Nationalists in China had big repercussions in Australia for decades to come. In the short term, we had here many people who thought that if the Reds did finally win in China, then they would be certain to press south, and work their way gradually to this fair nation, and thus gain Tasmania, which was clearly the ultimate goal. That was what America was preaching. **It was called the Domino Theory, and it said that all the goody nations of the world (US allies) had better club together and make sure that it did not happen.**

There were other people who said this Theory was preposterous, and that we should welcome the victory of the Communists in China, and that the Theory was far-fetched and ridiculous. In any case, they said, we were in a position to trade masses of goods with China, and we must ensure we became firm friends with them.

These events in China still had a long way to go, and we will return to them a little later.

CALWELL AND O'KEEFE

At the start of February, a photo appeared in the *SMH* of a woman with her children. The caption below it read "Mrs Anne O'Keefe, of Broadbeach, near Chelsea, Victoria, with her husband and five of her eight children. The Minister for Immigration, Mr A Calwell, has ordered them all to return to Indonesia by midnight on February 28."

This innocent-looking photograph marked the start of one of the major controversies of 1949. The story of Mrs O'Keefe was that **she and her husband** had been leading local fighters **against the Japanese in Ambon in Indonesia**. After a particularly successful attack, the Japanese were known to be coming to extract vengeance against her husband. **The Australian Navy was aware of this, and to remove her and her children from danger, evacuated her to Australia. This was in 1942.** Her husband was subsequently killed in action. She had re-married an Australian citizen in 1947.

By 1949, Calwell and the Immigration Department were well underway with their program of systematically kicking out those Asians who had been in Australia for a long time, and they came to Mrs O'Keefe, and thus she was told to leave and go back to Indonesia.

It seemed at the time, maybe, that Mr Calwell did have the right to expel them. **This nation clearly had a White Australia Policy (WAP) that said that no Asians were welcome.** It allowed for some rigidly defined exemptions, but these were for truly exceptional people. Calwell did not consider it at all exceptional that the lady had lived here for years, and had been married to an Australian for two years, and that the father of her children had given his life to fight against a common enemy. In fact, rather than seeing her as an exception, Calwell saw her case as presenting an opportunity to show just how stringent the WAP really was.

The WAP was not a policy that only Calwell supported. Indeed, most Australians at the time thought it was a good thing for most of the time. But **their sense of fair play** was violated by the callous attitude taken by Calwell in this instance. A large part of the population reasoned that the few exceptions would make no difference, and that Mrs O'Keefe had earned the right to stay in this country on humanitarian grounds.

> **Letters, Hope Power, Singapore.** An Australian citizen in Singapore, I am deeply shocked at the Press reports of Mr Calwell's callous and ruthless actions relating to the unfortunate lady, Mrs O'Keefe and her family.
>
> Already, the White Australia Policy has become a thing of ridicule and contempt in the eyes of the rest of the world. Must we, as sane-thinking fair-minded Australians sit down under the stupid, suburban small-minded bureaucratic actions of such people as Mr Calwell.

I can only hope that the public reaction in Australia will be such that Calwell will have to revise his dictatorial methods. I think that, with world affairs in the precarious state that they are in, it would behove us to cultivate the friendship of the "very" Near East rather than antagonise it. Possibly one step towards this would be to send a contingent of Diggers to help our Asian brothers combat the bandit menace in Malaya.

Letters, Roy Woodford, Singapore. For 25 years, I have worked and lived as a white Australian with Asians. As one who is respected by them and respects them, I say that the actions of Arthur Calwell have done the greatest possible harm to the future of relations with Australia and her Asian neighbours.

His latest outrage in the case of the O'Keefe family is almost the only topic of comment in the kampongs and villages in this country, and he has succeeded in stirring up such a hatred among these good people that even the Japanese could never have done. John O'Keefe was honoured for his work in the Allied cause, but **his family is not considered good enough to live with Calwell's "Master Race."**

Australia seeks the goodwill of her Asian neighbours. If Mr Calwell stays in office a feeling of resentment and hatred of things Australian will be built up among Asians. **Get rid of him.**

Letter, Iris Hyde. The bewildered citizen, trying to find his way amid the tortuous inconsistencies of our foreign policy, must come to one inescapable conclusion - that it is designed to win enemies and lose friends.

There is no question about the complete agreement of every political party in regard to maintenance of the WAP, which is based on economic grounds. But the deportation of the Malayan seamen, and the projected deportation of Mrs O'Keefe, both highlight the fact that we cannot afford a too rigid administration of that policy.

Harshness may not only cost the goodwill of our neighbours, but also markets necessary for the expansion of our trade.

We now have a matchless opportunity to capture new markets, and producers in this country will find it hard to forgive any Government which wilfully jeopardises future trading prospects; they realise a time must come when keen competition will make all lost markets a matter of bitter moment. In interpretation of the Immigration laws let us, therefore, exhibit tact, humanity, and understanding.

Overseas governments and others reacted strongly and negatively. Sultan Hamid II, head of an Indonesian State, said all Australians would be expelled if Mrs O'Keefe was deported. In Singapore, a British-owned independent conservative newspaper, *Free Press*, described Calwell as being bone-headed, a bungler and a misfit. "Seldom has a Government, whose declared policy is to seek the friendship of its Northern neighbours in Asia, allowed a misfit ministerial colleague to so jeopardise its aims." The Dutch in Indonesia, the Malayan, and Indian, and

Singaporean, and Chinese governments all expressed similar objections.

Did this deter Calwell at all? Certainly not. In fact, he went to his Canberra colleagues in the Labor Caucus, and asked for their opinions. This august body is made up of the elected representatives in the Parliament, and is renowned for its solidarity, and that means that it rarely rejects a proposal from a Minister. So on this occasion, Calwell got the unanimous support of Caucus, and thus emboldened, he was free to go on to excel himself.

On February 12, he announced that Mrs O'Keefe, who had been due to leave on February 28, would now be deported on the 22nd. **This was what was then called "laying in the boot."**

Menzies, the Leader of the Federal Opposition, always patiently waiting for someone to flay, now came to the party. He started by saying that he supported the WAP one hundred percent. But he took exception to the previous argument of Calwell that to allow coloured people into the country would lead to a "mongrel" Australia. He flayed the word "mongrel", and asked what type of person did Calwell have in mind that could take good Australians and turn them into "mongrels." He added, quite a few times as was his wont, that he considered Calwell to be unbalanced and deranged. He thoroughly enjoyed one of his many debating victories.

The *SMH* editorial of February 15 was quite emphatic in condemnation of Calwell. The WAP is now the subject of contempt and discredit, and this sorry affair has done nothing but add to that sorry situation. Calwell, by his references to "Mongrel Australia" and "Dutch trickery" has succeeded in offending both the Dutch and Indonesian governments at the same time, which is no mean feat since they are avowed enemies.

The *SMH* went on to say that Calwell's action in bringing forward the expulsion to the 22nd shows that there is to be no relenting. No matter how this case is resolved, the Australian government cannot win. The decision now to allow the woman to stay here as a gesture would allow us to gain back some credibility and repair some of the harm done by Mr Calwell's tactless blundering. But, the editorial goes on to say, it seems inevitable that the matter will now be settled in the Courts. Though, it adds, it would be deplorable if such a petty and indefensible action were forced into further prominence as a legal issue.

It did, however, come down to the Full Bench of the High Court on February 22nd to make a judgement. **The submission from the Crown** was that Mrs O'Keefe was a migrant, and was thus within the category of persons liable to be deported. **The submission for O'Keefe** was that she was an evacuee from the Dutch East Indies, and could never become a migrant, and was therefore not subject to the Immigration Act. Also that she had never signed an agreement to return home at the end of the War, and certain actions she rightly took to clarify her position at the time of her re-marriage stood in her favour.

Later in the day, debate centred on whether she was a migrant or a prohibited migrant, under various Acts, some of which had been changed in the middle of her stay. It was all very legalistic, and of course, there was no suggestion of granting her and her family leave to stay on humanitarian grounds.

On March 19, the Court voted by four to two in favour of O'Keefe. They also granted her costs. Mrs O'Keefe and her brood were safe from deportation. Calwell and the Immigration Department took the decision with the good humour that might be expected from them. They said that they were likely to appeal, with the spectre of huge bills facing O'Keefe if this time she lost. And **charmingly, they said that they would now investigate whether they could deport her children, without the mother,** because they might have violated some arcane clause that their mother had avoided by making various applications in her own name. Fortunately, neither of these events happened, and O'Keefe was allowed to slide into obscurity. The Immigration Act was subsequently amended to comply with the Court's ruling, but no further attempt was made to harass the O'Keefes.

Comment. The reader can see from the way I have presented the above description that I am opposed to Calwell's actions. I have to say that at the time I was just 15 years old, with an unusually strong interest in politics, engendered by what I saw as the injustices always foisted on to the coal miners that I lived amongst. Needless to say I was strongly Labor in my sympathies, and up until the coal strike of 1949 (see later in this book), I thought Labor could do no wrong.

But there was one Labor exception to this. I had a strong antipathy to Arthur Calwell. He, in my opinion, could do no right. I will not try to explain where this came from, and indeed, I do not think I could. Whenever he opened his mouth, I was always ready to rubbish him. I must add that every time now that I write of him, I have the same tendency. So please do not expect me to answer the question that I now pose to you. It is one that has occupied my mind many times over the years, and despite the research I have done, still remains unanswered for me.

Why did Calwell prosecute Mrs O'Keefe with such malice and vigour? On the one hand, was it because he believed that any deviation from the WAP would so dilute our blood that we would indeed become a mongrel nation? Was it because he thought that even the smallest deviation from blood purity would become the thin edge of the wedge? **It certainly was not that he had no element of humanity within him**, as can be seen by his actions in other spheres. Then why was he apparently so devoid of humanity in this and other cases?

On the other hand, was it simply the cold calculating view that the WAP was supported by a large body of voters, and that to be the rigid enforcer of it would win him popularity? Could he have thought that the average Australian did not differentiate between Asians, and "they all look the same to me", and that the hatred of the Japanese would carry over to all Asians? As he saw it, was he prepared to sacrifice the well-being of a trivial (Asian) minority in order to get the votes of a big majority of racist Australians? **To put it in today's parlance, was he playing the racist card?**

As I said, I do not have the answer. Various biographers touch on this question and come up with their own ambivalent answers. Perhaps you might like to get a couple of biographies and look for yourself. But one thing I can comment on is that Calwell was thereafter always followed, into any political forum he entered, by references to the O'Keefe affair. Just as Bob Menzies was always followed by calls of "Pig Iron Bob." The sorry mess might, or might not, have gained him some votes in the short term. But by 1960, when he was running for Prime Minister, and when public antagonism to the WAP was becoming dominant, references to Mrs O'Keefe did nothing to help his cause.

LIVING IN A DIFFERENT WORLD

In 1934, the British Colour Council, covering the entire British Empire, published a *Dictionary of Colour Standards*. This showed the 220 different colours that could be identified in producing silks, wools, bags, shoes and even lipsticks. So that if a merchant wanted to order a supply of an object, he could specify the colour he needed and the manufacturer would know exactly what to supply.

A Royal Tour of Australia had earlier been expected in Australia in 1949, but it had recently been cancelled due to the King's illness. This was disappointing, of course. But this was doubly so for the Colour Council because **it had planned to introduce four new colours to the world as part of the bally-hoo for the tour**. Still, the Council expected the pastel colours would be popular even without the Tour.

The colours chosen by the Queen were sky-green and Shetland-blue. Princess Elizabeth picked cherry-pink and primrose.

Other members of the Royal family had earlier launched colours, such as limeflower and linden. Elizabeth had supported princess blue and spitfire blue. The Duchess of Kent had selected marina green in 1931.

Comment. The British Colour Council was established in 1931. By the end of the 1960's it was mainly obsolete, though its standards were still used for some British Commonwealth flags, academic robes, and flowers and other horticulture produce.

INFANTILE PARALYSIS

Alaska had been free from white-mans' diseases since time immemorial, but had succumbed to TB and influenza in the 20th Century.

Now, the dreaded disease of poliomyelitis was appearing there. It is thought that a single itinerant man carried the disease to a number of areas. Of 60 Eskimos now showing symptoms, 13 have died, and 36 are paralysed. The Government is thinking about setting up special camps for the ill, that will isolate them, in much the same way as lepers' colonies were used in early days of the Century.

Comment. Australia did not know it yet but it too was about to suffer a polio epidemic. Throughout the 1950's, parents were frightened every time a child got sick. Many people succumbed to the disease, and some died, many were crippled for life, and a few spent the rest of their lives in an iron-lung.

In the 1960's, the Salk and then Sabin vaccines came to the rescue, and wide-spread inoculation programmes removed the blight from Australia.

MARCH NEWS ITEMS

Pre-War, one of **Sydney's tourist attractions** had been **the Archibald Fountain**, near famous Kings Cross. When war came in 1942, the water sprays were turned off to save water and electricity. Now, **seven years later, the water has been turned back on**.

The polo cross season opened in Sydney with a bang. We are told that the correct gear to wear this year is jodhpurs and shirts, slacks and skirts, or smart cotton frocks and sandals. One lady added **a swish bowler hat to her jodhpurs. The Committee said the hat was acceptable, and she was not asked to remove it.**

The Duke and Duchess of Windsor were back in London. You might remember that, pre-War, the Duke had **abdicated the British throne** so that he could marry the then Mrs Simpson, an American divorcée....

The papers say that their reception was "cool."

The battles between **surf-board riders and body-surfers** at Sydney's beaches continues. The latest tactic **of the riders** is to infiltrate the surfers and shout "Shark , Shark" and **this quickly empties the beach of surfers**....

Surfers have woken up to this, and are staying put when they hear the call. Authorities are worried that **when a legitimate call is made, it will be ignored**. Several Councils **are considering banning all boards**, especially at week-ends when the crowds are big. Riders are saying that if this happens, they **will just surf outside the flagged area. Talks are continuing.**

King George VI had been scheduled to visit Australia, with his family, this year. Sadly, he had suffered a series of illnesses, and **the tour was cancelled**. Our Government had ordered **six Daimlers to be used during the visit. Now, they idle**. An offer has been received for one of them from an Indian maharajah....

Comment. The cost to the public purse of the cancelled tour was never published.

Australia is not the only place beset by strikes. In New York, gravediggers have been on strike for seven weeks. They want six days pay for five days work. 700 bodies are piled up awaiting burial....

New York's famous Cardinal Spellman has organised for 100 students at a nearby seminary to join **the strike-breakers**, and dig graves. **This is a big political risk for a man of the cloth.**

The Council at Sydney's Rushcutters Bay have decided to allow sporting clubs to **use the Council's oval for Sunday sport**. Any code of sport will be free to tender for the usage. A condition will be that no fee is charged for entry, and that no raffles or fundraising will be run....

This is a controversial and provocative move. Churches are strongly opposed to Sunday sport. They say it will **desecrate the Sabbath**, and they fear that it will **decrease Church attendance**....

Gradually, **over many years, and many dead bodies,** Sunday sport became common. Then **much later, fees for entry, and professional players became accepted.**

YEAR OF THE RABBIT

Some people say that rabbits are cute. City children, travelling in the country, often exclaim "Oh look, Mummy, there's a rabbit", and Mummy usually slows down and says "they're so cute". Other people, in 1949, had a different view of them. They saw them as shiny skinned carcases that were thrown into the fridge or ice box, waiting to be stewed for the evening's meal. But another group, the farmers and graziers of 1949, saw them as nothing better than a plague that was destroying their livelihood.

The trouble here was that the little vermin ate the same food as the sheep, and were, at the same time, destructive to the pasture, because they scratched and dug into the soil. So, when a great plague of rabbits came to live on all sheep properties in Australia, it was at the expense of the sheep. This made the graziers hopping mad.

They tried to shoot them, but there were too many. They tried to trap them, but the rabbits could breed faster than the traps could. Fumigation and poisoning killed more sheep than vermin. Harrowing and digging up the land just put the land out of use for too long. Even the hungriest of dogs was no match for a few thousand bunnies.

The fall-back was to put up long wire fences, and to gradually clear paddock after paddock. But, alas, after the War, Australia was **still desperately short of wire netting**. Every grazier in Australia was crying out for netting, and every farm was faced with financial hardship as their sheep starved to death. So the pressure for "somebody to do something" spilled over into the newspapers.

The Land Editor of the *SMH* painted a solemn picture. He pointed out that this nation had 100 million sheep, but that the number could be halved in six months. It had become a battle between the sheep and the rabbits for every blade of grass, and the rabbits were usually the winner. **For every 100 miles of fencing needed, only one mile was being produced locally.** Some graziers had not been able to buy a roll in eight years.

He went on to say that "the grey army" was massed in denser formation than ever before known. One typical owner had poisoned, trapped and dug out tens of thousands of "the buggers", but as fast as he killed them, the paddocks were invaded by new hordes. Six-month old lambs were dying in droves because all the nourishing food had gone. In desperation he bought a huge tractor-ripper with which to tear the warrens and burrows to pieces. There was terrific slaughter. Every yard of ground was torn up, and the soil was littered with mangled carcases. But to no avail; the grey army kept advancing and the dead were replaced by new generations.

The Federal Government decided to act. On January 25, it had announced the expenditure of 100,000 Pounds on wire netting from the US. It explained that the only real solution was to increase wire production in Australia, and decreed that the new wire must be used for patching the official wire rabbit-proof fences that stretched right across areas of Southern Australia.

No one was impressed. Experts pointed out that the sum involved would scarcely make a dint in the problem. One Letter writer said that individual graziers would get exactly nothing, and that would have to be divided across all the other graziers in the district. He concluded that "nothing divided by fifty comes out very close to nothing, and that is a bit less than needed."

Others said that it was well and good to say we needed to increase production, but the fact was that there were not enough skilled workers in the nation to run the mills needed. Further, there was no accommodation for the workers when they were recruited from Britain. And even further, there were not enough steel rods to provide the material for the wiring, and that situation would not be fixed till late in the coming year.

The situation got even muddier when the wire-drawers and weavers, who produced the netting, protested against the importation because, it turned out, they were not getting enough work. This was because there were not enough wire rods, and this was explained in turn by the catch-all cry that there was not enough coal to produce them.

Letters, P Osbourne. I read with interest the Government's remarks relating to the purchase of wire from the US. Mr Pollard's views are typical of the thoroughly misinformed and unsympathetic approach by all members of Government of this country, especially those not engaged in land activities.

Mr Pollard makes the wild statement that if all the netting in the US were imported to here, it would not cure the rabbit plague, and that fumigation was the only effective method.

Without adequate and secure fencing, all of Mr Pollard's analyses are quite useless. Perhaps he does not know that rabbits travel away from most forms of attack, and unless they can be pinned down by fencing, they cannot be eradicated. His remarks on wailing producers are typically odious and offensive.

The *SMH* weighed in with a startling statistic. In an editorial, it said the dollars made available for the purchase of the netting were enough to buy 900 miles of it. The country needed enough for 300,000 miles. It also pointed out that the cost of the US wire was four times greater than that of the Australian product, and that the overseas product was greatly inferior to ours. The only real solution was for the means of production to be increased forthwith. Dollars had to be found by the Government to buy the milling machinery needed, and surely it would pay for itself many times over in a short period.

Comment. The War was over but its legacy of shortages of material and men was still evident, and of course **the well-developed skills of passing-the-buck had not been at all lost**. The truth is that the various Governments and large companies had had four years to anticipate this plague, and were only now responding to it. Chifley kept saying that we, as a nation, could not afford the dollars required to buy things from overseas, but on the other hand, here is a great example of lack of dollar allocation going close to wrecking an entire industry.

There seemed to be no short-term solution. The plague continued. The situation was alleviated somewhat in some areas when the February storms filled burrows with water, and drowned the kittens. Nature helped out again, for the moment, with the onset of winter. But there were **two other factors** that contributed more in the long run than the gradual increase in production of netting.

The first was the fact that plagues often stop themselves. It seems, maybe, that the population increases to the stage where Nature says that enough is enough, and sends out some diseases to stop the excess breeding. Whether or not this delightful technical explanation is correct, the population for the next two years was down somewhat on 1949. Not by a great deal, but enough to be noticed.

The second factor, a few years hence, was the introduction of myxomatosis. The disease may be related to the disease I described so learnedly above, but in any case, it worked. It killed huge numbers of rabbits, all across this vast pasture of a nation, and gave the farmer a few years peace.

As a Post Script, let me include **four items on rabbitty matters**.

News item. Rabbits are invading Sydney's inner suburbs. One has even been seen **in the city**. A Department of Agriculture official said he had seen one in the vicinity of the Queen Victoria statue, and around Hyde Park. Home gardens were under attack. It was suggested, **by a gentleman in a Homburg**, that this was the ideal opportunity to get rid of the neighbour's cats. He said that it was legal to poison or trap these rabbits, and who could be blamed if some unfortunate cats were killed in the process

There was also some meaningful progress with fencing.

News item. The first shipment of aluminium alloy wire netting arrived from Britain this week. It is as strong as steel wire, but is one third lighter than the steel product, and can be left in the ground without corroding. It can also be used in oyster beds. It will be allowed duty-free into the country.

Potted rabbit: Boil a rabbit until the flesh falls off the bone. Throw away the bones. Take the flesh, and put it through a fine mincer. Add the secret herbs that your mother entrusted only to her most handsome son. Mix thoroughly. Put out into bowls that have been well washed if they have been used for sanitary purposes overnight. Allow to cool for 12 hours in a refrigerator. Eat thinly sliced on toast. If you re-heat it too much, you might get a form of food poisoning that is often quite mild.

Letters, L Howell. Might I suggest to Mr Spooner and the Liberal Party that in addition to the rabbit pest another matter deserving their attention is the succour of those, who, like myself, have been the bunnies for so long.

I refer to those of us who have no powerful unions or associations to protect us from the ravages of whoever likes to attack us.

We pay our increased fares, we kow-tow to the publicans, we wheedle something from the greengrocer, we furtively and humbly approach the tobacconist and the fish merchant.

We pay our taxes in full, we pay increased admittance fees, and we accept the favours of taxi-drivers. We do all this simply because we can't do otherwise.

I understand there are approximately one and a half million white collar workers -- or rabbits in Australia. I feel we are being skinned just as thoroughly as our rodent brethren. Which party is prepared to do something positive for us?

ETERNAL DISPUTES OVER PENSIONS

If I had to, I could argue that the western world had come a long way in the last Century. But I do not intend to do that. One reason is that my statement would clearly be true for some matters and, just as clearly, not true for others.

In one area, though, the matter of **providing a universal pension for the elderly**, much progress had been made. Most people now agree that some pension should be paid to indigent and poverty-stricken elderly. This was not always the case. But what about those who were not really in financial difficulties?

Letters, Geo Stall. I am a man with family responsibilities and I not only have to contribute for my own superannuation when retired but the heavy taxation imposed means that I am also paying for the pensions of many **who never contributed a penny to their own pensions**.

Yet because I shall have superannuation for which I have myself contributed, I shall never be allowed to draw the old-age pension.

I am also certain a large proportion of those who draw the old-age pension and free social benefits had quite as good an opportunity in life to make some provision for their old age as I and thousands of others have had - but they let it go, not being prepared to make the necessary sacrifice.

Comment. These are arguments that have persisted right through to the present day. In fact, with just minor changes here and there, it could have been written by someone some 70 years later.

One side of the argument is that a person who has worked and saved, and paid taxes, for decades is refused a pension. **Whereas**, another person, who had done none of these admirable things, and has saved nothing, **does** now get the pension. What is the fairness, or the justice, in this, it can be asked? Another writer adds his voice.

> **Letters, D Watts.** We do not care for old people because they are virtuous, but because they are no longer able to fend for themselves.

They may not, in their time, have paid into superannuation funds, not having had the opportunity. But **they did pay taxes**, directly or indirectly, and benefits which the investment of those taxes brought are being enjoyed by younger generations to-day. Moreover, they, when younger, contributed to the education and keep of those who are being asked to help them now. Also, in one way or another they helped support those who were old or needy while they, themselves, were able.

It is not true that many of those old persons who now need help enjoyed opportunities to provide for themselves in their old age. **They suffered a Depression** in which the life's savings, investments, or small businesses of many of the thrifty people who were past their prime were swept away.

Comment. As I mentioned earlier, no one is arguing that no pension should be payed to the impoverished. **But what about the thrifty? Surely, it can be argued, they deserve to get back some of the money they have paid in taxes over the years.**

Then another, counter, argument comes into play. The **Government has only a limited amount of money** to dispense. Clearly, it is said, this should go the impoverished and not to those who will survive anyway.

Other arguments flowed into the Press. **Some young people** favour turning back the clock and say that no pensions should be paid at all. **Some charities** want no pensions, but hope that residential institutions be set up for the elderly.

Christians ducked the issue. How far should Christianity go? Should every person with wealth go so far as to give all that wealth to the needy? **The Communists** jumped into bed with this argument, and said of course all wealth should be shared equally. **Insurance companies** claimed that proper insurance policies can be devised for everyone.

People in the country pointed out that few of them had any scope to join a super fund until the last year or so. If they had been frugal all their lives, how come they could not get the pension all of a sudden? **People on farms** complained that their various assets precluded them because of the farm and assets tests.

The argument went on and on, right up to the present day. On this issue, all the voices in the chaos of democracy have been heard and can still be heard.

Looking back, a few facts are clear.

Firstly, old people are better off than they were in 1949.

Secondly, every five years or so, the Government or Opposition announce plans to **change super**. There is no coherent policy that guides people in planning their lives.

Thirdly, there is no doubt that there **has** to be **some** limit on what is paid out. But the argument over just where this line is will never be solved by Political Parties devising policies in the shadow of an election. **If we ever grow up** to the stage where **our Representatives can talk sensibly to each other**, then we might be able to find a common philosophy that will guide policies and rules.

AUSTRALIA'S DICTATION TEST

This test was based on the Immigration Act of 1901. It gave the Minister the power to deport certain people at his whim. It was used regularly to re-enforce the WAP, or as a threat to force compliance.

It did not mention colour or nationality. It said the Minister could ban "prohibited' persons, and there were certain types that were thus defined. If you were a criminal, or a properly certified idiot, or a carrier of communicable diseases, then you might start packing your bags. **You could also become prohibited if you failed to pass a language test.** This clever little device, lifted from Natal in 1897, required a person to translate a passage of over fifty words, dictated to them, into English.

The problem was that the passage could be in any language at all. So, **the administering officials simply chose a language that they suspected the person did not know, and off he went**. If a person passed, they could keep going with different languages till they got him. Egon Kisch, notorious in Australia in the 1930's for his Communist sympathies, passed one such test in Scottish Gaelic, but failed the next.

This test was not applied to Mrs O'Keefe, because her status was different. But clearly, the whole thing was devised to keep out anyone the Minister thought inappropriate, and was the standard threat to force compliance in the deportation of hundreds of Asians at the time of O'Keefe.

As you would expect, **the Asian countries resented it enormously**. They saw it as just another trick so that the white guys could say their skulduggery was legal.

Comment. No person was known to get through the full exam period.

ENVIRONMENT ISSUES

Most of the nation's electricity came from the burning of coal. Hydro and oil were just starting to get a foothold. Also, there was no national grid for electricity, so that every State Government had its own power stations, sitting somewhere nearby.

Needless to say, all of these pre-war units were creaking at the joints, and badly needed upgrading. The Letter below describes the situation around Sydney's major site.

Letters, P Bryant. While the majority of Sydney's residents are concerned about the continuity of Bunnerong's supply, we who live within a two-mile radius of the power station share this uncertainty and also suffer from the filth that emanates from its many chimney stacks. The whole countryside is being inundated with black, oily grime.

Women in the locality on washing days have to be conversant with wind variations to prevent the possibility of having to rewash clothes. Paintwork is ruined and windows have a continual oil smudge. Grass and other vegetation is covered with this filth, which adheres to boots and shoes and when carried into the house causes ruin to carpets and other floor coverings. Market gardeners in the vicinity have whole crops of spinach and lettuce completely ruined, not to mention the damage caused to flower growers who specialise in white flowers for cemeteries, etc.

If it is not soon remedied it will give this area the appearance of a mining town.

Comment. Letters such as this, that took a **community** viewpoint, were rare. People collectively were suffering from so many blackouts, and so many restrictions, that they **had no concern for environmental niceties**. If you woke up and found that you could not boil an egg, or if you could not cook your steak and chops at night, you did not worry about pollution. And again, if restrictions said you could not have hot water in the mornings, or run radiators after nine in the evening, you cursed the government and you did not worry about how **green** your valley was.

This type of thinking dominated society. Let me give you a silly example. At one stage, Bondi Beach in Sydney was flooded with swimmers from all over Sydney who wanted a swim. They bought their lunches at cafes and shops along the beachfront and after eating a healthy meal of fish and chips, went back to the suburbs leaving behind great heaps of newspapers all along the beach. The daily papers were full of complaints from the residents and shopkeepers. The local Council reacted and said it would provide more inspectors to police the area, and give fines to the villains.

No one at the time suggested that the solution was to provide more bins for the wrappings. In fact, there were no bins at all along the waterfront. It was a bin-free area. No one thought that it should be otherwise.

The same attitude prevailed everywhere throughout society. Forests could be destroyed for so-called progress, ovals could be alienated for bowling greens, wetlands could be filled for housing, roads could carve up forests.

At this stage, **the rare environmental protests came from just a few zealots, individuals who worried about the future and thought that their protests could make a difference. But there were few, very few, organised groups that raised their voices.**

They would come after the entire society had become a lot more comfortable and could turn their thoughts towards

collective efforts and resistance. That started in earnest about 20 years down the track.

Comment. It is all different now. Vocal Greenies pop up all over the place.

LETTERS TO THE EDITOR

Comment and opinion.   In 1949, if you got cranky and wanted to write a Letter to the papers, you needed pen and ink, a blotter, a decent light, stamp and envelope. Then most Letters were rejected by the Editor.

Now, in 2019, you can stand on a street, and Twitter to the world. And all such writings are published. Unfortunately, many, many people do this. One result of this is that a Letter to the Editor has lost much of its punch.

When a Letter now goes to a newspaper, it carries **a little** weight. **But only to those who still read them.** But even here, the quality of Letters had fallen a lot. Most Letters now are vicious missives saying "gothcha", or you changed your mind in the last thirty years. Or spiteful envious complaints. Clever little Letters have vanished altogether, as have creative, thoughtful messages from well-meaning and balanced writers.

If this worries you at all, you could of course write a Letter to the Editor. But better still, I suggest, you could write your own book, and sneak your concern in somewhere.

But, no. No one would do that. That would be too devious for words.

APRIL NEWS ITEMS

The Labor Government **drove another nail into its electoral coffin today** when it announced that **petrol rationing would continue** on over the coming months.

Various Federal and State Ministers met last week and decided that **they would no longer set the prices of new cars**. This meant that manufacturers could set the prices, and that market demand would force them to modify them. This would allow the haggling, discounts, and bargains across many dealers that we are now very familiar with....

Motorists welcomed the changes and were relieved that the artificial prices and the heavy regulations on buying a new car would be lifted. But, **they should not celebrate too early**. On April 1st, Governments announced the changes would be delayed **at least until April 29th**, when a new conference would be held....

It seems that some Ministers are having second thoughts because they now think that the **prices might jump** a lot if restraints are lifted. **We will have to wait and see.**

The Electronic Delay Storage Automatic Calculator, a British invention, can make 100,000 calculations per minute. EDSAC has 1,000 valves and 32 four-foot long mercury tubes. This machine, and a few others, were **the forerunners of the computer revolution** that has obsessed the world ever since.

The Grand National Steeplechase race for horses was an annual event. But a special one that excited the

English. It was an extremely long race, about 4.3 miles, in two laps, and horses needed to jump over about 30 barriers and water jumps in order to finish....

This year, **43 horses started**, but most came to grief at the barriers. **Only 11 finished** and a few were destroyed on the track. As a consequence, **protests against the race** started to become very much louder....

But to no avail. The race continues to be run to the present day. It was first held in 1839, and is now a British institution.

Melbourne, April 30. It was officially stated that the 1956 Olympics would be held in Melbourne. It was chosen in the fifth ballot, when Buenos Aires was defeated. In the prior ballot, Los Angeles and Detroit lost out. Melbourne won by 21 votes to 20. **It is the first time in history that the Games will be held in the Southern Hemisphere.**

Our new aircraft carrier, *HMAS Sydney*, was built in England and has done her sea trials there. This extensive process took about 9 months and up to **800 Australian sailors have been stationed on her. Another 700 British sailors** have joined the Oz Navy, and they are all set to sail her home to Australia ....

Our sailor boys have not been idle in the Mother Country. **40 of them have married rosy-cheeked Pommy girls.** These young brides will not come home **with** their hubbies. They will be given top priority for urgent passages under our Migration scheme.

THE SHARKEY CASE

The Communist Party in Australia in April, 1949, was an offshoot of the Russian Communist Party. As you will remember, this latter group had staged a revolution in Russia in 1917, and had seized power. From that time, the spectre of Communism had haunted the Western world, which did everything it could do to bring about its downfall. But to no avail.

When World War II came, Russia entered on the side of the Allies after some dithering, and emerged from that conflict as one of the victors. But its moments of glory were short-lived, and **by 1949 it was competing with America all round the world to see who could build up the bigger sphere of influence.**

The Australian Communist Party meanwhile was a registered political party, and regularly contested elections with, at their best, less than a third of the success the Greens have ever got. In other words, they had no **political influence. But** they had also exploited worker demands for better wages and conditions, and had thus gained important positions in the Trade Unions. Here they were influential. They were well organised, they had a legitimate cause, and were quite happy to use cunning and bully-boy tactics if needed. So, many of **the most important and belligerent Unions in this nation were under the spell of Reds**.

The rank-and-file were different. They all wanted to improve conditions, but most of them voted Labor, and only a few voted Liberal and Country Party. However, the members of the Communist Party presented a different population. Granted some, perhaps half, were happy to achieve change through democratic and parliamentary processes. **The other half, however, wanted to get the changes quickly and through revolutionary means.** These were the firebrands who stirred the passions of other workers, and persuaded them to strike. These were the people that governments throughout the Western World wanted to silence.

Mr Laurence (Lance) Sharkey was one such person. He was Secretary of the Australian Communist Party, and was not frightened of voicing his opinions. **The Labor Government** at the time was under great pressure to do something about the large number of strikes, but **was reluctant to somehow penalise its friends in the Trade Unions.** But Sharkey was not in any Union and he was an executive of the constantly reviled Communist Party. He would be a great scapegoat if he did or said anything untoward.

Well, he did just that in March. He was rung by a reporter from the *Daily Telegraph*, and was unwise enough to say the following.

If Soviet forces in pursuit of aggressors enter Australia, Australian workers would welcome them here.

Australian workers would welcome Soviet forces pursuing aggressors just as the workers welcomed them throughout Europe when the Red troops liberated the people from the power of the Nazis. I support the pronouncements made by the French Communist leader, Meuren Chevez.

Invasion of Australia by forces of the Soviet Union seems very remote and hypothetical at best.

I believe the Soviet Union will go to war only if she is attacked. I cannot see Australia being invaded by Soviet troops.

The object of Communists is to struggle to prevent war and to educate the masses of the people against the lies of war. **The Communist Party also wants to bring the working class to power and if factions in Australia use force to prevent the workers gaining that power, Communists will assist the workers to meet force with force.**

This message was delivered over the phone, without prior preparation, and to a reporter who would presumably only use those bits that he thought newsworthy. So, it is quite garbled, and a bit random. The *Telegraph*, always delighted to rubbish the Communists, thought it had a good story here and went to print with the complete text.

The Federal authorities jumped for joy, and yelled "Gotcha!" as they issued a summonses against Sharkey. The charge was that in saying these words, he had committed sedition. This seemed an unlikely charge since he had not blown up or burned down any Parliaments, nor had he urged anyone to do so. He seemed to have just made a series of juvenile statements that were to be expected from any self-respecting firebrand. The gentlemen issuing the summonses, those protectors of free speech, **could have heard some real sedition any Sunday afternoon down in Sydney's Domain if they wanted to.**

The Communists were shocked by this charge. They called meetings of several committees, and the resolutions were, of course, that various Unions would call strikes if the summonses were not withdrawn. The Unions themselves were a bit of a disappointment. For example, the three main Miners' unions disassociated themselves from any such strikes. On the other hand, the Waterside Workers were all **for** a strike, and called for the arrest of Bob Menzies instead of Sharkey. The Union movement was split right down the middle on the issue. This, of course, delighted the Sydney newspapers.

For a few days, Sharkey went missing while the Federal Police tried to issue him with their warrant. But, in due course, he re-appeared after "a holiday at Terrigal" and was charged under the Crimes Act.

At the start of April, Sharkey went before the Special Court. His counsel sought dismissal of the charges on the basis firstly that it was not clear that Sharkey had uttered the words. Nobody believed that. The other grounds for dismissal were that **he had expressed no intention to act seditiously, and that even if he had done so, the proposed action was not seditious anyway**.

By now the case was getting bogged down into technical legal arguments. But, later in April, the Court decided that he **did** have a case to answer and that he should be sent to trial. We will meet up with him in a few months' time.

Comment. I expect that many readers will not find Sharkey's words seditious, under the common meaning of the word. There can be no doubt that because of his influence on the Union movement, and because he was at the forefront of much strike activity, he was carefully selected for prosecution. Had he just been an ordinary citizen spruiking at a political meeting, he would not have warranted attention. This seems an odd way for British justice to work. But it still works that way, I think. For example, at the moment in 2019 you are more likely to be charged with certain crimes if you are Arab than if you are not. **Our systems for security always get a bit perverse under stress.**

CROWDED PLACES

Travelling in 1949 was not as easy as it is now. Most families still did not have a car, and even if they did, petrol was still rationed and was in very short supply. For a city-dweller and his family to go to some major holiday event, it usually meant making the sandwiches and packing up the night before, then leaving home fairly early the next day, and proceeding via a number of different modes of public transport until you got there. From Seaforth to a Sydney race meeting for example, it meant a bus trip to Manly, then a ferry ride across the Harbour, then a tram or bus to Randwick, or perhaps a train ride to Rosehill. Public transport was no better than it is now, and so half the day was spent in waiting for connections.

I think people were a lot more patient in this regard than they are now. They were also more tolerant of conditions. The trams for example, in holiday mode, were often severely over-crowded, with passengers hanging off the boards and crushed into the racks. Trains from the country were filled like sardine tins, with people standing between the seats in dog-boxes. The platforms outside the carriages proper were crammed with hardy souls, who simply coughed and spluttered, but never complained, when they went through long tunnels.

On the other hand, when they got to the sporting event, the fun started. **There was no one at the gates waiting to pounce on any grog they were carrying.** There was no metal detector, or frisking of the two-year olds and everyone. At the Sydney Cricket Ground, there was a spacious grassy Hill, **instead of the horrible concrete monstrosity that is there now**. There were no security guards lining up at twenty-yard intervals round the ground at any stoppage in play. And the Sydney Ground was fenced with white pickets, rather than the heap of flashy billboards and junk that have replaced it. **I will stop. I am back on the "good old days" theme.**

But let me add, that there was no music, so-called. Between events, you could talk to someone near you without having some ear-piercing drongo scream words of love or hatred alternatively at you. **No. No. I really will stop.**

Where were the crowds going? At this stage I will not talk about where they went prior to April. Except to say that they had gone to the beaches in droves in Summer. Some of the ladies in neck-to-knees, some at the other extreme in the very new bikinis. Baskets and tablecloths were everywhere, because there were no Esky's in those days. Likewise there was very little in the way of sunscreen, and those sea-shirts of later years were still absent for children. Hats were acknowledged as a good thing, but everyone's concentration dropped off, so that, for example, no one wore them while in the water. So everyone got burnt to a crisp. A few days later, there might have been the occasional bronzed Anzac body, but that night, there were only burnt and sore shoulders and legs by the million.

After everyone had been grilled enough, the family made the tortuous trip home, only the baskets were a bit lighter. The lucky kids went straight to bed. The unlucky ones were coated with damp baking soda which was supposed to help with the sunburn. That was one of those really stupid old housewives tales round. Anyway, a good time was had by all, and when the real sunbathers could move again, they normally started to think about their next jaunt.

April 1949 was a time of big crowds. Of course, by then cricket had finished, and Rugby League and AFL had started. **Rugby Union** was hanging round in the background, but that was in those days just an amateur sport for those from university and GPS schools, and **played by toffs who couldn't tackle**. But, here, I will look at other crowd-drawing events that drew large numbers.

Sydney's Royal Easter Show had been re-vamped after the War, and was now a big attraction. In the last week, daily crowds of 50,000 were common, and the usual brilliant agricultural products and displays, and the wonderful animals, were there for all to see. The tree-chopping remained a crowd favourite, and the Grand Parade brought in the numbers. Fairy Floss was also excellent that year, and so too was the boxing in the Boxing Tent, and the show-jumping. Merry-go-rounds kept the little ones quiet, while the horse-o-plane did the same thing for those a bit older.

For teenagers and young lovers, there were various forms of Dippers and Ferris Wheels, that raced round the sky at night, and some boys had a big thrill as petrified young girls saw their chance, and flung themselves screaming into innocent arms. There was always the adventure of going to the toilet, and most people still remember **that** stench any time they come across a similar situation now. In all, it was jolly good fun, and in spite of the travel time to get home, off to bed happy, and this time, without the sunburn.

The GPS Regatta. The Greater Public Schools were, and are, an Association of the most influential, and rich, and prestigious, and pretentious, and valuable schools in Sydney. Every year they still hold a regatta for their oarsmen to compete over a programme of about eight races of various shapes and sizes. The ultimate race is for the big boys, and is called the Head of the River. Whatever else the winning school does that year, when it wins the Head, it has crowing rights until the next time.

The race is held on the Nepean River, around Penrith. In 1949, public transport to get there was limited indeed, so buses hired for the day filled part of the gap. But, being from GPS schools, the families of the students mostly had cars, and so the many parking areas were filled to capacity. That year, the crowd that attended was estimated to be just short of 20,000. This is an enormous number, given the number of students actually at the schools. It shows that in those days, interest in the race was widespread outside the

GPS school system. Rather sadly, I think, this interest has since lagged, and the event passes without much more than token interest.

For the record, in 1949, Shore won the Head by a quarter of a length from Newington. The Cox was B Haydon. By now, he will be aged about 87. If you meet or know him, you might like to congratulate him.

ANZAC Day, April 25. In 1949, the crowd that watched the March in Sydney was 200,000. This is a lot of people, and it was repeated in every city in Australia. And it was repeated in every small town and regional centre. You can make a guess at what the total was across the nation, but it comes to a staggering number.

Just as significant was the range of people who marched. Firstly, there were Diggers and others from two World Wars, and the Boer War. Then there were police, firemen, nurses, town bands, school children, football clubs, Unions and professional associations, and more. The Trade Union Lodges and their colourful banners brought some old-world spectacle to the scene. Just about every group in the community took part. It was truly a spectacular vote of thanks from this nation to it heroes.

Comment. As the years have gone on, for a time the numbers watching, and the numbers marching, have fallen, and so too have the number of outside organisations who march. I know it is inevitable that this will happen as the Diggers gradually die off, but still it has made me sad now and then.

But, I am happy to note, that over the last few years the numbers attending and marching have both started to increase again. That means that the youth of today are realising the great sacrifice that these fine men made for them, and that they appreciate it in a tangible way. What a wonderful thought. Do not let anyone convince you that our current youth are as shallow as we were. They are not.

The racetrack. Racing was more popular with the general public than it is now. Attendances at meetings were larger, the number of people betting was greater, and the public interest in racing was much greater. Newspapers carried much more racing news than they do now, and there were always heroes and villains, both equine and human, who were sanctified or vilified by the alert public. **Granted, there were in effect no totes available, and betting off the track was not legal.** But there was a well-organised and readily accessible network of SP bookies that made **the joys of illegal gambling available immediately to every home in Australia**.

If you are wondering **what you should wear** to your local 1949 race meeting, let me advise you. **Feathers. Undoubtedly feathers.** They are the accessory of the year. On your shoulder, clutched at the waist, on your head, on the hat on your head. If you want to be fashionable, you must wear feathers.

Comment. Women can wear them too.

MAY NEWS ITEMS

Rationing of sweets in England officially ended today. In London suburbs, queues started to form as early as seven in the morning. Little confectionery shops round the country were full all day. The Food Ministry had asked adults to wait a few days, but 90 per cent took no notice of this. Many shops were sold-out by mid-day....

This was **the first day in the lives of many children that they were free to buy lollies without government restrictions**. Strict **controls had been introduced nine years earlier,** and had been retained through the War and ever since.

A slogan for Road Safety groups at the time was *Death is so Permanent.* **It tells an obvious and sobering truth.** It was pushed endlessly when I was a teenager, with graphic images of death and the devil and it is the only one I remember. **I would like to see it used again.**

There were millions of young **orphan children** living in terrible conditions **in Europe.** People here were starting to talk about how they could bring some relief to them. Various Societies had **wanted to bring 10 of the children here as a sample** and have them adopted by local families. It was hoped that this sample could be expanded to larger numbers if it succeeded. But **this idea was scotched** as the Government showed a lack of genuine interest....

Britain too had a host of orphans. Our regulations said they could come **only if they went to blood relatives**

living here. Overall, a large number of adults were willing to adopt, but **regulations and administration** were stopping the flow....

New Zealand, in the meantime, **had a regular quota of 100 British orphans a month** landing there.

The war of words goes on. For a couple of years, the bad **Russians have been blocking radio propaganda** into Russia emanating from Britain and America. But technology has moved on, and for a time, messages can get through. At the same time, **broadcasts from Russia to the good guys** can also get through to Britain. **Much celebrating on both sides,** though what effect it had on anything is hard to measure.

Forgotten special activity on Mothers' Day. Phone services were brought to a standstill across the nation as huge numbers of children rang Mum. **Trunk calls** were especially hard hit, and callers had to wait for hours in many cases....

Crowds visited cemeteries, bearing white flowers.

The Victorian Government will set up **a Royal Commission into Communism** immediately. This is the **beginning in Australia of an obsession with the Reds** and what they might aim to do in Australia....

But we are not alone in this. In particular, similar, and **more extreme ideas are developing in America**, and soon Senator Joe McCarthy will be conducting his **nefarious campaign against all things Red** in Hollywood and the USA.

HAPPY DAYS ARE HERE AGAIN

Prosperity is here now. The *SMH* on May 3rd published a review of how the nation was faring economically. It found that, after coming out of the Depression, and then fighting a War for six years, and then suffering four years of soul-destroying austerity, this nation "presents a truly remarkable picture of prosperity." It pointed to a range of statistics that confirmed this, and gave some of the reasons for it. It said that there was full employment and that there was adequate capital around to make things happen. **Indeed, it said, the main problem was a shortage of men and materials.**

Then it went on to expound on a list of its perpetual hobbyhorses. It flayed the miners for striking, it disliked the 40-hour week, and it was wounded by the "tendency to slackness" seen in strikes that lead "to the rough corrections of a Depression."

Overall, though, times were good. Far better than they had been for over a decade. And, if I might get ahead of myself, over the next few years they got even better. Australia was shaping up for one of its economic booms. And hand in hand with that, but for even longer, came the Baby Boom.

Chifley, however, was not impressed. The Prime Minister said in Parliament that the buoyancy in the economy **would not result in an end to petrol rationing**. Arthur Fadden, the leader of the National Party, had been campaigning for weeks to have rationing removed, and it was time for Chifley to rule out this idea. He argued that Britain and the Empire were still short of dollars, and that this situation would continue, despite the fact that all countries therein were recovering economically. He was not impressed by the fact that Britain had recently doubled its petrol ration to individuals, and that some Empire countries had removed it entirely. He was conscious of the need to maintain dollars, and even if petrol could now be bought from non-dollar nations, buying from that source ultimately cost us dollars.

Chifley had only that week been described overseas as a "miser". Here, even among Labor supporters, he was often referred to as a kill-joy. He was now sticking to his oft-used mantra that it was sinful to spend dollars to make dollars, and in the face of vast public opinion, refusing to free up petrol.

W C Wentworth was not impressed either. He was a Liberal Parliamentarian, and well known for his fiery utterances. These were sometimes profound and some bordered on ratbaggery.

Letters, W C Wentworth. We need a positive approach to the petrol problem, in place of the negative and hopeless attitude adopted by the Prime Minister, Mr Chifley.

He tells us that the removal of rationing would cost us fourteen million Pounds a year; but, apparently, he has failed to realise that the secondary effects of this rationing, cumulative now over four years of peace, are resulting in a dollar drain far in excess of this figure.

Petrol restrictions, with their inevitable effect on rural life, are responsible in large measure for the **drift away from the land**, and the poor figures for food production. The amount of butter and meat thus lost far outweighs the fourteen million dollars "saved" – and all food production can be reckoned as "hard" currencies in international trade today.

If Mr Chifley really wants to get dollars without doing damage, let him concentrate on coal production. A few million tons of extra coal, for instance, would enable freights to be hauled by rail, instead of oil-consuming lorries over long distances. Or it would enable us to produce an extra 500,000 tons of steel, and these are worth much more than fourteen million dollars in hard currency.

The petrol story does not end there. In a few months, we will have another intriguing installment.

FOREVER AMBIT CLAIMS

This prosperity brought out the first of the really serious **ambit claims for wage increases** that entertained the nation for the next 70 years, and have persisted even today. An ambit claim is a demand, in this case by a Trade Union, for a wage increase that far exceeds any amount that any sensible person would expect. In our centralised wage-fixing system, where all electricians across the nation were supposed to get paid the same rate, regardless of how profitable their employer was, their Trade Union would every few years make a claim to some tribunal for a wage increase for all of these bright sparks.

The tribunal would sit for a few days or weeks, deliberate for a few more, and then give an increase of three per cent per annum. But before that, the interested parties, the bosses and the Unions, would tell the tribunal that the nation would plunge into disaster, or that the workers would all die, if such and such a rate rise was not forthcoming. There was always a lot of blustering and pathos associated with this show, and **the ambit claim** was part of this.

On May 18, the ACTU came out with a claim that the basic wage should be increased to ten Pounds a week. Now given it was currently set at six and a quarter Pounds, this represented an increase of sixty percent, and was clearly in the category of an ambit claim. The Union movement hoped by setting its claim really high, that as it got whittled down bit by bit, they would end up with a little more than if they had gone in with a reasonable claim. Of course, the learned tribunal knew all about this, and in this case, like all others, the pay rise was fixed at three percent. But, in the long run, this spectacular claim set the tone, and the practice of ambit claims continued well into the future.

END OF THE ROAD FOR TRAMS

At about this time, various mutterings suggested that the people of Sydney, or at least the mutterers, were ready to get rid of their trams.

Letters, J Keane. The report of the London transport experts was rather substantially devoted to the aspect of making the tram system pay. I think there are broader aspects worthy of very close study, and I think if examined in true perspective, should dispel any remaining doubts about the efficacy of buses.

Basically, the tram is much the same as it was twenty years ago. Improvements have been effected, but the future holds no promise of revolutionary change unless it is in terms of cheaper power.

This cannot be said of buses. We are all aware of the advances made in construction and mechanical efficiency in the past twenty years and the future holds promise of even greater improvements in the future. I have in mind the gas turbine engine which, when fully developed, should revolutionise mechanical transport.

Buses equipped with such a power source will have **a smoothness of operation** comparable with an ocean liner, and operation and maintenance costs very much reduced.

The *SMH* agreed. Under the heading, "The Hazards of Tram Travel", the Editorial of May 19th pointed out that last year 187 people were injured by tram travel. It said that tram **smashes** had also been high, with eight already reported so far this year, and that four of them had been collisions with other trams.

The Transport Department had a different view. It argued that given the mileage travelled by trams, "percentage of accidents was almost nil." And it pointed to a recent **crash of buses** where one of them actually ended up on its side.

Still, the pressure to **get rid of trams** mounted and, within a decade and a bit more, the tracks had all been covered with tar, and the tram sheds at Bennelong Point were being magically transformed into an Opera House.

AUSTERITY WAS NOT IN SHORT SUPPLY

Having painted a fairly rosy picture of the economy, I think it proper to point out that all of the problem associated with the War had not gone away. These two small examples will serve as reminders.

The first one shows that blackouts could be expected at irregular intervals. They were caused by a shortage of coal, strikes by operators in the powerhouses, breakdown of equipment, hot weather or cold, or height above sea-level. Likewise, their duration was uncertain, except to say that they always lasted long enough to spoil the evening meal.

The second example is a plaintive letter from a visitor to our shores.

Letters, A V, At Sea. Our tanker recently discharged a full cargo of petroleum of various kinds at Sydney after a voyage of 29 days from the Persian Gulf.

Imagine our dismay to learn that not a single bottle of beer could be obtained, in or out of bond, because of strikes etc. For consolation, we were told that even a large passenger steamer, just leaving for the UK, had been cut down on its beer requirements.

We are only rather unspectacular tanker men, but does it strike you that if we, or our kind, do not come to Sydney then large passenger steamers will have no need for beer, for they won't be able to sail, and those motor runs into the country will be a thing of the past.

Meanwhile, the large passenger ship, with many Sydney folk on board, sails for the pleasant climate of an English summer, complete almost with beer, while we return to the hottest place in the world to fill up again, most probably for Australia, absolutely dry.

BUNDLES FOR BRITAIN

This remarkable scheme had been in operation for five years. Under it, Australians could send off a big package of goods to people as a gift to help their relatives, or friends, or perfect strangers, to survive the horrors of war and its aftermath. The contents of the bundles were tinned meats, condensed milk, syrup, dripping and the like. They were enormously popular in Britain, and the receipt of a bundle was always a cause for rejoicing in the starving nation.

Now, five years after the War, Australians were still sending in huge numbers. **Thirty thousand were sent a week in the first three months of 1949.** It was an incredibly large number, because they were not cheap, and because of the administrative difficulties that were always put in the way.

On May 1, another foul-up started to appear. British authorities advised that racketeers were moving in, and dummy persons were receiving large numbers of these parcels. This meant that the goods came into Britain duty free. The Brits were suspending the service until they got it sorted out. This was the second such interruption already in this year, and the patience of the senders was being sorely tested. In fact, these delays were the thin edge of the wedge, and after this the scheme went downhill. But it still remains as an act of national generosity that it is hard to surpass.

THE FALL OF SHANGHAI

By May, 1949, the Red Army had moved from Nanking to the outskirts of Shanghai. They had no resistance on the way, and thus arrived rested, and with all the armament they could want, and were ready to fight. From the outskirts of the massive city they bombarded a few places, fought a few skirmishes, and then marched into the city virtually unopposed. The retreating Nationalist Army left just ahead of the incoming Communists, so that the looting by citizens that normally occurs did not happen.

The city was virtually undamaged, and there was almost no fighting in the main business and residential areas. Shops had re-opened and people were going about their business as normal. The feeling of trepidation felt previously had given way to relief, because at that time the Nationalists were saying that they would defend the city, to the last drop of their blood. The *SMH* Editorial remarked that the hardest part for the conquering troops was to fight their way though the multitude of Communist flags that welcomed them.

Editorials said the victory marked the end of serious fighting in China. The Revolution was now here to stay, and this opened up a number of questions for Australia. We needed to ask ourselves whether we will recognise China? And, a separate question, will we trade with it? There was always the question of how China would behave in the future. Would it settle down peacefully, and be content with its neighbours? Or would it follow the Russian Communist line, and try to gain converts by force?

Then there was the question of the **Nationalist Army**. It was now in disgrace, pushed out of the main areas of commerce, but still huge and capable of much violence. Would it re-form and attempt a comeback? Could the individual soldiers simply go back home and settle down? This seemed unlikely, given that they would go back to areas held by Communists.

There were more questions, about Chiang Kai-Shek, the Nationalist leader. In January, he had offered to resign if peace could be gained as a result. Then he went out of sight. No one believed he was gone for good. When would he re-appear? Would it be as a peacemaker, or as a warrior once again? The bets were that he would not think of going quietly into retirement.

Finally, there was the attitude of the Unites States. It had supported Chiang obliquely for years, and desperately wanted the Reds to lose this War. What would it do now? Might it even intervene with armed forces of its own? Probably not, but surely it would not stand by and watch China become yet another Communist state?

So, a lot of questions were asked. Of course, many of you readers know now how much of this turned out. But at the time, the whole matter was a great mystery, and the subject of much debate. The biggest burning issue of the world stage was how far the Red menace would spread. There were a lot of people here who indeed felt threatened by this menace, and were about to incorporate this into their political stances.

In the meantime, the masters of the Liberal Party, whether they were genuinely concerned or not, realised that here they had a recognised and vilifiable enemy that they could use for political purposes. They were able to do this for the next twenty years. After the fall of Shanghai, the Reds were forced even further under our Beds.

BERLIN BLOCKADE ENDS

After the War, all of Germany was divided into four sectors. The goodies, Britain, America and France, each got one. The baddies, the Russians, got the other. Berlin was **the big capital city, so it too was divided into four sectors**. The problem was that it lay within the Russian sector of Germany proper.

So the other three sectors of Berlin were hemmed in by Russia. Back in June 1948, the Russians cut off access to these sectors from the outside world by closing all roads, rail links and canals, and leaving only three air corridors open to Allied entry.

It was then that the famous Berlin airlift started. The Allies, particularly the Americans and British, carried all supplies, for a city of 2.3 million people, into that city for a period of 11 months. The air corridors were crowded with planes that landed every few minutes. The whole point was to show the Russians that, whatever tactic they came up with, it would be countered by the Allies.

Moving forward into 1949, on May 5, after a period of negotiation, it was announced that the blockade would end on May 12, 1949 . The Allies said that they would continue to send material into the city to act as a stockpile in case the blockade was re-introduced. Other than that, the matter appeared to have been settled amicably, and for a few days it was thought, quite wrongly, that this marked the beginning of a new era of co-operation with Russia.

News reports, May 12. Berlin is the happiest city in the world today. People are rejoicing the fact that street lights will be on again at nights, that evening tram-cars will be running again, and that fresh potatoes will now be available. After months of austerity and shortages, after months of scepticism that a solution to the blockade would not be found before the Allies tired of it, the city is now celebrating, and the whole city is lit with jubilation. Great crowds are greeting every Allied vehicle with cheering, and painting signs among the ruins that say "hail to the new era" and "Berlin lives again".

General Lucius Clay, the retiring US Military Governor in Germany, said that "the end of the blockade does not just mean that trains and trucks are on the move again. It has a deeper significance. The people of Berlin have earned their right to freedom and to be accepted by those who love their freedom everywhere."

But despite these reports, the Berliners were not all that optimistic. They were **still occupied by their victors**, and in fact would remain under them for another forty years at least. Little did they know it, but a great divisive Wall was later to separate them from their countrymen, and an economic divide just as great would plague them all. It took many years before that once great nation was back to normal, and indeed, in the case of East Germany, there are many who say it still has not yet made it.

GREETINGS FROM ABERMAIN

Abermain, as you doubtless know, was a small coal-mining town of 2,500 people set in the middle of the Cessnock coalfields. To me, at 15 years of age, **it was clearly at the centre of the universe**, and nothing else that happened in the world mattered much.

Still, I might talk about some of the utilities we lived with, to give you a little reminder of what most of nation was like outside of the cities.

Of course we had no sewer. Just a dunny up in the back corner of the block, as far as possible from the house. My family had a brick structure, but all others were timber. We were somewhat special in this, and so we were always looked up to.

We had running water too. Half the population also had it. But our neighbours next door had to survive off a tin tank and hopefully a lot of rain. In dry spells, one of the five girls next door came daily to our back door and asked could she please have a bucket of water.

In our street, there were about 100 houses on each side, strung out along a gravel road, with wide frontages with lots of gates for horses and cows to travel to and from the essential paddocks. Four street lights were scattered along the one-mile length of the street and we had no trouble with cars at night, because coal miners had no cars, so that there were only four in the whole town.

But there were no crimes in the region, so people could walk on the footpaths at night, though they had to be careful of the cyclists who always preferred the footpaths to the road.

People riding at night had no lights, and this was because there were no still no bike-lights after the War, and because they were all lawless cowboys.

Walking on the **roads** at night was too dangerous. They they were man-traps when dry and deep lagoons in the wet. Still, once every year they were graded level, and this brought relief for a few days if it did not rain.

Community activities were well catered for. The Star Theatre showed a double feature movie twice a week. The local Plaza Hall ran old-time dances every Saturday night, and either housie-housie or a Talent Quest on Fridays. Occasionally, they were able to fit in a night of Community Singing on Thursdays, a very popular event among the oldies. Can you remember *In the shade of the Old Apple Tree*, and *I Love You Truly?*   And what about the war-time favourites *Oh, Johnnie, Oh* and *Daisy, Daisy, Give me your Answer Do?*

To round out the societal scene, I add that all the major Christian Churches had their own following, and attendances on Sundays were pretty good. Sermons were mainly as boring as they had always been, though occasionally the odd priest or vicar railed against the tolerance the miners collectively showed towards Communism. No one took any notice.

The town had a pub on top of the hill, and one at the bottom. This latter venue was celebrated in the district as a fighting pub. It sold Resch's beer, and this was regarded "as a fighting beer." On Friday nights, when a half a million thirsty miners with a fresh pay-packet squeezed into the front bar, you could guarantee a dozen fights, by 10 o'clock. Of course, six o'clock closing just meant that the front doors were shut. The back door was always open, while the beer lasted.

Sporting events had a great following. The local sporting field, **behind the bottom pub**, was filled with spectators who came out to cheer on the Rugby League team or the cricketers in various local derbies. This field was also the eventual destination of the Anzac Day and the May Day and the St Patrick's Day marches.

Comment.   Looking back, it all sounds quite primitive. And, indeed, it was. But no one in the town knew **that** then. We were an isolated town, no one ever left, and no one in their right mind ever came to stay. We had no ambitions, no outside civilising influences, no reason to travel, and no money to do so. So, in our ignorance, we were quite a happy town.

Give or take a few details, I think that much of country Australia was just like that. But even blissful ignorance had a use-by date, and that reality came home for these miners when automation allowed the removal of pillars from the mines, and when open-cut extraction destroyed the countryside and brought moonscapes to vast areas of the beautiful bushland.

JUNE NEWS ITEMS

During the War, the trotting industry was banned from holding **night meetings**. This was, it was claimed, because the nation could not afford to use all that electricity for trivial pursuits....

Now, this ban has been removed. From here, **night trotting started to boom,** and for the next 30 years, Friday night trotting, boosted by radio broadcasts, excited punters across the nation. Of course, off-course betting was illegal. But so too, the pubs were **supposed** to be shut at six o'clock. Still, **a night at the local, drinking gallons of beer, and picking winners**, kept many a man and woman off the streets on Fridays.

In middle June, **a boxing match** between **a young Aboriginal called Jack Hassan**, and a world-famous Frenchman, Andre Famechon, was fought at Sydney's Stadium. The local lad had a win, and the fight drew a lot of attention because the Frenchman behaved so badly after the decision....

But I mention this here to draw attention to **the public's great interest in boxing as a sport** and for gambling. This was before the world boxing scene had degenerated into chaos, and people could still believe that Champions had truly earned their Titles....

This nation was about to become excited, for a couple of decades, by names such as Dave Sands, Freddy Dawson, Jimmy Carruthers, and Lionel Rose. Radio networks again played their part and this time, it was **Monday** nights that regularly kept the punters guessing....

A third sport that gained great support at this time was wrestling. This had already **descended into the ridiculous**, with numbers of hulks claiming to be the World Champion, and the events clearly **scripted** by management, and hammed by giant actors....

In Australia, we got most of our draw-cards from America. And despite the above faults of the sport, it was great watching. I can remember a night at Sydney Stadium when Chief Little Wolf put his famous **Step-Over Toe Hold** on a hapless local, and held it there while the helpless opponent screamed for minutes in (mock) agony. What a great way to spend a Tuesday night....

Finally, in this sporting spree, I should tell you **that tennis was also enjoying a nation-wide renaissance**. The pre-War giants, Bromich and Quist, were being rushed off the net by youngsters like Sedgeman and McGregor, and Davis Cup broadcasts over the three days of New Year held the nation spell-bound....

Of course, this was in the good old days when only amateur players were acknowledged. Any person who wanted to be **paid** for playing was regarded as a pariah, and was not even allowed to practise with an amateur....

But soon, American Jack Kramer would break out of this mould, and he formed his troupe of professionals that toured the world. It took 20 years, but now we have professionals dominating in all major events.

FAIRFAX VERSUS McGIRR

The NSW Labor Caucus approved changes to the electoral laws in order to suppress all radio and newspaper election comment for the two days prior to and during the election. Their claim was that the newspapers were in the hands of capitalists who constantly besieged the readers with anti-Labor propaganda, and generally swayed the electorate from the facts, with distortions in the news and in editorial comment. The news blackout would give citizens a period of two days for calm reflection.

The *SMH*, all guns blazing, of course took up the challenge. It attacked the decision on the basis that it was a violation of free speech. "The gagging of Press and radio for **three days** is just as much the invasion of a fundamental democratic right as if the term had been fixed for **three weeks**." It went on to caution that we were heading down the path of last year's Czechoslovakia, and both Hitler and Stalin were lucky enough to get a mention. The Communists were singled out for a little more. "If the McGirr Government was wholly in the pocket of the Communist Party, it could not have devised an attack on freedom more agreeable to the enemies of democracy."

The editorial was rich in its prose. It talked satirically of the "big bad newspapers coming out on election morning and scaring the timid sheep with stories of Socialist wolves." It talked about the Labor Party wanting to put their coverage over to the back page, and there to print it in invisible ink. It closed with the statement that these new measures show just how fearful the government is, and - in the obligatory shot at the Communists - how much these latter villains must be delighted.

The Premier, Mr McGirr, was quick to respond. He stated that for as long as he can remember, certain newspapers have specialised in last-minute election attempts to discredit Labor, and confuse the issues. These attacks have been made **at a time when "it is impossible to answer them, before the poll**, and Labor is always at the mercy of papers which almost without exception are antagonistic to Labor." He argued that this is why he was insisting on a reasonable period of reflection, so that voters can sit down calmly and make up their own minds.

Then he really laid the boot in. He went on to issue a prepared statement to say that to describe the daily Press as free is completely misleading. All the daily newspapers in Sydney are absolutely controlled, and controlled by a mere handful of individuals – the Press proprietors.

He averred that the papers are **organs of propaganda, just as they were under Goebbels**, and the only difference from Goebbels was that here control was in the hands of six persons rather than just one.

Warwick Fairfax, writing as the "Chief Reporter" of the *Herald,* apparently thought that them's fighting words. He opened with "The Premier speaks of this paper as an instrument of propaganda, just as it was under Hitler and Goebbels. This is a wicked and vindictive lie, and the Premier knows it to be so."

In a special feature article, **he attacks the proposition that the paper was guilty of bias**. He points out that over many years the *SMH* had gained a reputation, both at home and abroad, for presenting both sides of the story; that it gave equal space to both Parties on all matters, and that frequently it put Labor's own arguments into its editorials. Indeed, he says, if it did not do this, it would certainly lose many readers, because half of them were Labor supporters. He talks about the affront it was to the journalists of the paper who were free from direction, and who prided themselves on their impartiality.

He goes go on to remember that Labor had made various attempts to start up its own Newspapers, and all of these had failed. Most of this money has been thrown away on useless strikes, and he added, never forgetting he was a good capitalist, "served only to glorify Union bosses and to serve the evil ends of Communism".

Then he changes tack. He talks about the dangers of politicians, presumably Labor, stomping the country just before an election, and being free to spread rumours and make all sorts of promises, without the Press to expose them. He adds, concerning the propaganda charge, that if this were indeed true, then this criticism of his paper would never have seen the light of day. Indeed, "the Herald generally makes a point of printing attacks on itself."

McGirr would not be silenced. A few days later he continued his attacks and added that the NSW Opposition, led by Vernon Treatt, can have an open go right up to within two days of an election. "They have perfect freedom to criticise, distort, and misrepresent until 48 hours before an election begins. However, we believe that an interval is necessary to permit a bewildered people to consider the position calmly, undeterred by last minute forays and alarms."

Well, I imagine you think that this intriguing little skirmish has ended. But, no, you are wrong. It was only half way. A week later, **Mr McGirr stepped back in again**. He argues against the impartiality of Fairfax's papers. He asks whether the man in the street thinks them unbiased. On the contrary, he says. Most people consider the *Herald* to be partisan with just plain propaganda, and take that into account when they read it. The comment you can hear almost everywhere is "You can't believe what you read in the newspapers." Does he think it is possible for Mr Fairfax himself to be the judge of this? "After all, few men are able to recognise their own species of biased opinions."

McGirr claims that the legislation bodes ill for the Liberals. This is proved by the depths to which the *Herald* is going to spike it. Then, he scores, or thinks he does, a juvenile point. He points out that his original letter was one half-column, while Fairfax's reply was five columns. This is pretty weighty stuff. He adds a few references to Mr Fairfax's having reduced discussion to the level of vulgarity, and talks about the latter's mendacious political humbug.

Everybody stand back. **Here comes Fairfax.** He firstly returns to the autocrat theme, and how his paper had served the nation over time. "When Hitler came to power, the German consul accused us of publishing propaganda, not news. Communists today accuse us of publishing propaganda, not news, about Europe today. The Premier implies that our news columns are generally propaganda. Time will always uncover the truth."

He then outlines six instances in Parliament that week where it was the *Herald* that was maligned, and so no one could lay the claim that it itself was the maligner. He concludes, with the now-familiar call, that the only protection against last-minute smear campaigns, say in marginal electorates, was to allow the papers to publish it as such. Inter alia, he added his own little bit of pettiness by stating that his own first retort to McGirr actually might have been spread over five columns, but in running lengths, it added up to two columns, not five as McGirr had claimed. So there, get that up ya.

So ended the open warfare. It would be wrong to think it went away though. Throughout the upcoming campaign, McGirr kept up his reference to the cupidity of the press, and how it was giving a distorted view to voters. Why wouldn't he? For many of his followers, he was talking to the converted. On the other hand, the Fairfax Press never let up on talking about the undemocratic dangers the legislation represented, and how Hitler and other charmers were just round the corner.

For the record, the legislation was passed along Party lines, and McGirr narrowly won the elections in June the following year.

Personal Comment. I think that it is a good idea to have a news blackout before elections. It gives time for voters to sort out fact from fiction, and to think about long term things that matter, rather than spur of the moment antipathies.

As far as the dispute between Fairfax and McGirr was concerned, to the average reader it was fun while it lasted.

It is not often we see a public display of such childishness from eminent public figures, and it is nice to see that they are just humans like the rest of us.

PETROL RATIONING ILLEGAL

On June 10, **the full High Court declared that Federal petrol rationing was illegal** under the Defence Act. The Court unanimously held that, four years after the War was over, restraints to further the war effort were no longer valid. Thus it declared that controls under the Act had to lifted and the sooner the better.

Of course, this was **welcome news to customers**. First and foremost, ration coupons were no longer needed, nor of any use. It seemed to mean that a motorist could go to a garage and buy as much petrol as he could afford. In some places, **for about half a day this did happen**. "Come and Get it. Bring your drums," customers were urged.

Reality was quick to set in. In fact, the Commonwealth still had **the only power to import petrol**, and if they chose to restrain supply, then the same amount would come into the nation, but there would be no system of sharing it out. But the Commonwealth was not clear on this at all. Chifley was concerned to keep the spending of dollars down, and wanted to bring in the same amount as before the decision.

Putting that aside for the moment, where would the system to regulate supplies, to share petrol equitably, come from? The most obvious answer was the States. But, on reflection, they wanted none of this. They knew full well that petrol rationing was really on the nose with the people, and they were not going to take the suicidal step of introducing it into their own States. Also, there was the problem of State boundaries. What if the price and method of rationing varied from one State to another? Surely, there would be an influx of motorists into the more lenient State, and that would place an unfair burden on the natives of that State.

For example, Canberra was still a Territory under **Federal** jurisdiction, and could in fact continue with the old system of rationing. If it did, would it result in a daily rush to or from the Territory to get the goodies? For a week, everyone sat blinking at the light. One thing became more certain. The Federal Government would do little to help the States set up their own systems of rationing. It said, mischievously perhaps, that it would contribute to the costs of any State which did re-introduced coupons, provided it was under the Commonwealth's control.

After a week of fumbling backwards and forwards, and telling each other not to panic, the Premiers agreed to meet to seek a common solution. The Prime Minister co-opted the meeting and they all met soon after. The Prime Minister confronted the Premiers with what he saw as the reality of the dollar-drain situation, and **said there was no hope of his increasing the flow of petrol into this country**. So, there the matter rests for the moment. Everyone was meeting every one, Premiers were not going to commit suicide and introduce rationing, and Chifley would not let any more petrol come into the nation. **What a ghastly mess.** How was it solved? Was it solved? We will come back to it a little later.

THE SHARKEY DECISION

Were Sharkey's careless words seditious? When he said, "If Soviet forces, in pursuit of an aggressor, entered Australia, Australian workers would welcome them. Australian workers would welcome Soviet forces following aggressors just as the workers welcomed forces of the Red Army when they liberated the people from the power of the Nazis", and a few other statements, did he commit sedition?

Well, **a jury sitting in the Special Court found that he did.** The defence argued that he had made no appeal for any person to do anything. He asked for no action from any person. But apparently, sedition was **what was in his mind** when he made those statements, so the jury found him guilty. The judge instructed the jury that Communism was not on trial, and they should get rid of negative images that they might have had of Reds. But to no avail, and he was found guilty, and bailed pending a sentencing hearing at a later date.

This was a shock result and it undoubtedly rocked the Communists, and also many unionists who saw it as an attack on free speech. It would have been a sensation at any other time. But a Royal Commission in Melbourne had just opened to investigate Communism and that completely stole the headlines. On top of that, the famous miners' strike of 1949 was on the very brink, and left no room for anything so minor as a ground-breaking sedition trail.

Two months later Sharkey was sentenced to three years in gaol. It was later reduced to thirteen months.

THE 1949 MAITLAND FLOODS

At the end of June, black nimbus clouds came in low and fast from the South for a week over the "cities" of Maitland and Cessnock, and the heavens opened up. I lived in a small mining town of 2,500 people at the very centre of the universe, I believed, in a place called Abermain. This nice little peaceful place was on a railway track that joined the two cities, on a stretch of rail privately owned.

The floods came suddenly. We were sitting in school, and one of the monks entered to tell us to evacuate immediately, because a flood was coming, and the last train out to Cessnock would leave in twenty minutes. We whooped with delight, and ran the mile to the station. We climbed into our dog boxes, and marveled at how lucky we were and thought what a great thing floods were.

The train took off, and got to East Greta and stopped between stations. Then it waited. Many of our schoolmates were serious idiots, and knew nothing of danger, so they got out to find out what was happening. They came back and said that massive Tester's Hollow, now four hundred yards ahead, was filling up with water, and the lines were covered. We waited while someone somewhere did something, and then our idiot scouts came back with the news that the water in Tester's was now one hundred yards away and looked to be lusting for human company.

After five minutes of rising and racing water, the train seemed the only one that could make a decision, so it crept slowly forward into the water. Its wheels started to slip. But it made some headway. All of this time, the depth of the water was rising. Then the wheels would not grip at all, and the train's wheels spun and spun. The water was still rising. It was now nine inches deep inside the carriages. If it got any deeper, the engine's fire would go out, and the 200 passengers would end up in a watery grave.

Now in case any readers are starting to worry about me, you can take it easy. **I did get out all right.** And the remarkable thing was that we schoolboys never had a moment of fear. We should have. People in all of the other carriages were scared to death. We could easily be stranded on the bridge, and then washed off it to certain death. But the schoolboys, idiots and others, simply knew that this was just a lark, that nothing serious would happen, that "she'll be right, mate".

Anyway, the train started to reverse, and by some miracle the wheels got traction, and we backed all the way into Maitland. There, we caught emergency buses via the back-roads to the coal fields. The rail-track was closed for seven weeks, and that meant I had to go to Cessnock High for that period. There, **I was the invisible man**, and I understood the feelings of those Poles and Balts that I described earlier when they came to my school.

That railway should have been hauled over the coals for this episode, but it didn't happen. I suppose that, being a private railway, it was not under the same scrutiny as a public one would be. Needless to say, Maitland was devastated. Then over the next seven years, it was hit by flood after flood. It was a repetition of the Biblical seven years of plenty – of rain. Since then, it has grown into a genuine city, and is looking exceedingly prosperous. Let's hope it never gets another flood like the one in 1949.

JULY NEWS ITEMS

There is a lot of talk about the possibility of **power strikes. But don't worry about it.** *The Sun Herald* this weekend will feature a supplement that will provide recipes for meals designed for **cooking with emergency gas or electricity....**

"Complete meals that can be cooked in a gas oven, pressure cooker menus, and recipes for **a triplex** and one-pot meals, that can be cooked over one gas burner, an electric hot-plate, or on a primus, kerosene or other emergency cooker." A free cooking time-table will be provided for use....

Does anyone remember what a triplex is?

In South Africa, Britain's influence is on the wane - as it is all over the British Empire. A bill will soon be introduced to remove the Union Jack from the flag, and *God Save the King* will no longer be the National Anthem....

These moves are not stemming from a rising tide of black nationalism. Rather it is coming from Dutch resistance to British rule. **South African nationalism will not really start to fester for another 20 years.** And apartheid (the separation of the population into blacks and whites) continued on for another 50 years....

Nationalism in the British colonies at the moment was showing up everywhere. The old maps of the world, showing British territories **in triumphant pink,** were about to be re-drafted over the next few decades.

A Melbourne man was driving his horse and cart along a road when the horse shied and threw him off. It then bolted, and the man chased it for 300 yards. As he caught up, he fell into the path of the cart. **It ran over him and he was killed**....

Horses were still a much-used form of transport across the nation, not just in the countryside.

Trams in Ireland's Dublin are to be replaced by buses. It was planned that bands and marchers from Unions and military would precede the last tram through the city, and every one would have a nice parade. But this did not happen....

Crowds of youths and girls took over the trams, and tore out the upholstery as it moved along, and then removed the fittings for souvenirs.....

All of Australia's cities are talking about **removing their trams.** Some will simply bury the lines, others will lift them, but in any case, they will go in the next decade....

And, I might add, **they will come back again in most cities about 70 years later.**

Noah's Ark is proving elusive. One Turkish exploration party claims to have found it in **the North**, and another says it has found it in **the South**. Meanwhile, a party of four Americans are seeking permission to climb Mount Ararat, confident that the Bible has given them sufficient leads to **go directly to the Ark without much searching**. As one journalist wryly wrote "all they had to do was look in the Archives."

THE MINERS' STRIKE

Big trouble had obviously been brewing for weeks on the Cessnock coalfields. For years, the shortages of coal had been a pain in the neck to Sydney and elsewhere. People were constantly confronted with blackouts, and shortages of gas, and other annoyances like restrictions on radiators and toasters, and on street lighting. Ships and steam-trains were often idle because of shortages of coal, and industry could not make the materials, like bricks and wire netting, that it was capable of doing. At that time, **Mr Chifley** visited the Northern coalfields around Cessnock, and told the miners that he was doing a good job on their behalf, and to stop asking for so much. He came away "disappointed", and at that stage, I believe, **decided to break the Communist influence in the miners' unions**.

At this point, I need to give a brief and simplistic explanation of how these unions worked. Every man who worked in a pit belonged to a union. For example, electricians belonged to the Electricians Union. The electricians from all the pits in a region had their own system of picking delegates to represent them at regional committees, and these latter lumped together to form a National Committee. **At the top of this pyramid for all Unions was the Miners' Federation**, and this group brought all these delegates together, and got sense out of them. And within the Federation was the Central Committee, who had the ultimate executive power.

It all seemed so democratic. Every worker, no matter what his job, thus ended up represented at the national level. Surely, that can't be bad. Well, Mr Chifley thought it was. He believed, along with almost everyone, that the power in the miners' unions had gone to the Communists right across the system. Most of the active delegates were Red, as were the active members on the Committees. And the Central Committee, of about a dozen men, was almost completely Red. The Communists had a stranglehold on the Federation.

Chifley now reasoned that this group had been causing problems for too long, and were never going to change. He was very conscious of an election looming in December, and reasoned that **if he beat the Communists in a big fanfare strike he would gain electoral support**. He knew that he would lose some miners' votes, but there was no chance that he would lose any seats. The miners always voted too solidly for Labor for that to happen. So he went home, and spent two weeks deliberately strategising.

The so-called cause of the strike. The third major player in the strike, after the Federation, and Chifley and the Government, was the Joint Coal Board, and its industrial tribunal, Mr Justice Gallagher. He was empowered to arbitrate between the Federation and the mine-owners over disputes, and to make awards over pay rates and general working conditions. He was the industry's trouble-shooter.

At this time, he was sitting on a log of claims from the miners for long-service leave. He argued about some parts of the log, as he always did, and the Federation gave two weeks' notice that it would call a general strike, of all mines round Australia, if their claim was not met by then. This type of posturing was pretty standard, and the normal practice was for the newspapers to get some headlines out of it all, and at the same time the interested parties would find a face-saving way out of the apparent impasse.

Early action. The strike started on a Monday, and **on that day** the NSW State Emergency Cabinet Committee decided to cut country rail services from the present 50 per cent to 15 per cent. They warned about disaster in everything else, talked about mass lay-offs of workers, and generally set the mood against the strikers.

The Federal Government, showing Chifley had not wasted the two weeks, on the Monday night sat until 2.30 a.m. to pass the Emergency Powers Bill which **froze the funds of all Trade Unions in Australia**. This included the miners' Unions, and other richer funds - sympathetic ones likely to help out the miners. This Bill meant that miners would not be able to get strike pay, and meant that in the long run, **they and their families would be starved out if necessary**. This Bill, at one stroke, ensured that if the Government made no mistakes, the miners would lose the strike. **It earned Chifley the hatred, unanticipated, of a million unionists round Australia. After all, the right to strike was guaranteed by the Constitution.**

The Leader of the Opposition, Mr Menzies, naturally supported the freezing of the funds. The question, he asked, was **what else** was the Government going to do. He suggested importing coal from overseas, but more realistically, he liked the idea of open cuts. Of course, going underground was too dangerous for untrained men, but surely open cut mining was just a case of gouging it out. He was completely wrong here, but the idea became a popular one, and popped up a lot a few weeks later.

Most other Trade Unions offered little support to the miners. Indeed, they could not do much, because they had no funds available to do so. And they were also precluded from raising any new money. But the truth was that most other Unions, whether Red or not, were not sympathetic to the miners. After all, when the miners went on strike time and time again, it was other Unionists who had to walk to work and eat their cold evening meal in the dark. Other Unionists, unless they were Communists, were fed up with the miners.

So, the miners quickly became isolated communities, beating a slowly dying horse, and running up a big debt with the local co-op store. They hated doing this latter, and so did their wives. They knew, and their wives knew, that a percentage of them would be dead or maimed within a year, and their families would be left on a below-subsistence pittance. So the households in the coalfields lay awake at night and worried about their mounting debts, and cursed the Baron Browns and Ben Chifleys who were the cause of all this misery. To the miners, this strike - and all strikes - was not primarily about money. It was about working conditions. They just wanted to live that extra ten years, with all their limbs working, that other men lived. To them, the evil plots of the Communists were just a beat-up by the Press and politicians. Such ideas were so preposterous that no one could take them seriously.

What happened next? Mr Chifley apparently discovered that there was about one month's normal supply of coal "at grass", that is, lying about at pit heads, already in skips and railway wagons. This made something of a mockery of all the emergency rationing that the States, especially NSW, had been doing to put pressure on the miners. But, in any case, he started to talk about "lifting" this coal at grass. However, he decided, not just yet. The miners still had some fight in them and this might lead to **forceful** intervention. So the idea was shelved for the time being.

Immediately the strike was called, officials of the Ironworkers Union and the Miners Federation went to the bank and withdrew sums totalling about forty thousand Pounds. The idea of these officials, Mr McPhillips and Mr Grant, was to get the money out of the banks before it was frozen. They succeeded, but they ended up before the Arbitration Court in a ton of trouble. They each refused to divulge the location of the money, and would not reveal where their account books were currently hiding. They were ordered to cough up the money and the books by 11 a.m. the next day. At that hearing, it was announced that about six others were similarly involved. Some of those involved were absent and their whereabouts unknown, and some of them refused to take oaths. Ultimately, John King, of the Western district of the Federation, was sent to gaol for one month for contempt of Court. He had refused to answer questions posed to him. That night, another 14 officials of the Federation, and the Steelworkers' and the Seamens' Unions, were issued with summonses for similar offences. The Unions also lost several appeals against the legality of the Act enabling the freezing of funds.

Call for nationalisation. After three weeks, various politicians came up with a shrewd call. They started to talk about nationalisation of the mines. This had been done a few years ago in Britain, and it was not popular among the miners there. The threat here was that if the Government could not get control of the miners now, then it **would** get such control if every miner in the nation worked for the government, and the government owned all of the mines. It could then dictate all aspects of mining, including whom it could hire and fire. Of course, this was an idle threat, because nationalisation on such a scale takes years, and would have had several legal challenges to face. Yet in the near-hysterical environment of this strike, it succeeded in frightening some workers, who of course opposed it. But it was supported by the Communists, who welcomed any nationalisation schemes. In short, though completely specious, it drove some wedges between workers on the one hand, and Communists on the other.

In the fourth week of the strike, the President of the Miners' Federation, Mr I Williams (no relation), and the Secretary, Mr Grant, (mentioned above), were each sentenced to 12-months' gaol, and summonses were issued against 23 other Communists. It appeared that the Court was getting fed up. The Chief Judge Kelly said that Williams and Grant "had set themselves up against the Tribunal, the Government and the law. You must not be surprised if the law fights back against you."

Coal at grass. In the fifth week, the various Governments were under the gun to get the strike over. Now it was not just the hapless consumer who was complaining, but industry was also. The solution was simple. Firstly, more coal at grass was found, and in fact so much was found that some restrictions even on civilians were eased. Funny that, maybe coal was not in such short supply as some people had thought. Second, all sorts of authoritative figures started talking about the need to move it, and how bad it would be if violence ensued. It was brain-washing, with the intention of getting the public to abhor any thought of militancy well in advance.

But, perhaps that was not the end of the matter. Mr Chifley and the Minister for the Army, Mr Chambers, plotted the next move. They decided that, **if union labour would not move the coal, then the Army would do so**. Their meeting was conducted with high secrecy, and thus guaranteed that everyone was well informed of it. So a few days later, when NSW State Rail started moving trucks parked near Rothbury, the miners, to quote the *SMH*, showed little interest, and the movement was one hundred per cent peaceful. In fact, the unions had decided quietly that they themselves should move the coal at grass and so get some money flowing again into the mining community.

But that was not the end of it. At the end of July, in a piece of high drama, **all police leave was cancelled**. Squads of police were sent from Sydney to the northern coalfields, and it was announced at the same time that **the Army was also on its way**. The reasoning was that if the unions decided not to load the coal at grass, then the police and troops would be necessary to quell the riots when the troops took to loading the coal.

This was quite dramatic, but quite silly. It was all posturing. The Government wanted to be seen as tough and decisive, and ready to meet brute force with greater force. There was no need for this. The miners had no history of violence.

The last time they had been violent was at Rothbury almost thirty years before when troops had shot and killed one miner and wounded others. **Every man in the pits knew the story of Rothbury, it was part and parcel of their being.** They now had no appetite at all for any repeat, and the Cabinet's posturing at this time was just a lot of theatrical humbug.

Even the *SMH* saw through it publicly. It said, "The recognoiterings and consultations have become so detailed and exhaustive as **to border on the comica**l. They did nothing at all for a fortnight, except hope that they would not have to do anything. Then, they began a series of staff conferences not unworthy of the preliminaries to a Combined Operations raid in war-time."

The strike was now six weeks old. The miners had had enough. The rank and file wanted to call it off. At the Lodge level, delegates were getting their instruction to sue for peace. The problem was that to do so, they had to go upwards to the Central Committee. But this Committee would not call any aggregate meetings of all persons so that votes could be taken. Some individual lodges flamboyantly held public meetings to vote for a return, but still the Communist Federation executives would not recognise the cry from below. For example, the front page of the *SMH* reported that on July 2nd:

A meeting at Singleton voted for settlement of their claims by the tribunal, Mr Gallagher, and the calling of aggregate meetings.

ALP speakers were cheered when they urged to end the strike, at Singleton, Muswellbrook, and

Swansea. When Communist Henry Scanlon tried to talk, he was hooted, amid cries of "We've had the Coms. Get out."

This mood was common across the mining towns. It was now only a matter of time.

In one last-ditch attempt to confuse the issue, the Federal and State Governments now decided to put the troops into open cuts. **This at least gave the miners a good laugh.** It is true that, for a week, it is possible for non-miners to go into an **open-cut** and scoop up coal that is lying round waiting to be loaded. But as soon as overburden has to be moved, or as soon as there is a need to work out what bit of coal to take next, then proper miners are needed for safety and for production. The troops went in with a fanfare, but sadly for the Government, there was no armed opposition. Then they produced lots of coal, and there was talk that they could teach the miners a thing or two.

After stalling, the Communists agreed to aggregate meetings, and the miners voted en masse to return to work. The police packed up and went home, the soldiers did likewise, and so too did the politicians. The miners went back to work, and Sydney got its gas and electricity and trams back. The Union officials who had been gaoled found the money that they had been hiding, and admitted to the Courts that they had seen the error of their ways. They now realised that the law of the land was more important than the rules of their Union, and were sorry for the contempt they had shown. They were released from gaol, and the fines they had paid were refunded.

Summing up. For Ben Chifley, the strike was a triumph and a disaster. He had achieved what he had set out to do. That is, **to break the power of the Communists in the miners' Unions**. But, apart from his first bold move of freezing Union funds, he had been slow off the mark, he had appeared reluctant to move decisively against Unions, and he had been altogether too theatrical in some of his later moves. He had lost many miners' votes, and this did not worry him. **But he had lost the votes of a million Unionists, who always remembered him as the man who froze Union funds, and left families to starve.** That is a heavy load to carry, and he and the Labor Party carried it for decades.

The miners came out of it, as they always did with strikes, a lot poorer. But a few weeks later they were granted the most generous long-service leave terms of any Union in Australia.

The Communists suffered a major loss. They had succeeded in their exceedingly short-term goal of disrupting the nation, but they had now lost a great deal of face, and they subsequently lost their positions - for a few years - in all sorts of Unions, not just mining ones. But, it must be said, they made a comeback a few years later. Still, they were no closer to getting acceptance at the ballot box. They just could not get the vote. The people here did not want revolution. The radical ravings of the Communists were seen to be just that – ravings.

AUGUST NEWS ITEMS

The City of Grafton on the NSW North Coast is all excited. It had been granted a licence to hold the **National Marbles Championship for this year**, and it expects to host it into the future. The Licence has been granted by the Greyhound Public House in Sussex, which has controlled the event in England since 1932....

In 2019, Grafton has lost the licence, and the contest is now held **annually in the NSW city of Parkes** at the end of March.

The *Sunday Herald* will publish its annual Supplement this weekend with information on everything you need to know about Knitting with Wool. These instructions have proved very popular in the past, so to avoid disappointment, you are advised to **order your copy** "before the Paper sells out."

Britain's "most notorious killer of the Century", George Haigh, was executed at Wandsworth Prison. He was **found guilty of killing nine people**, and he claimed to have **drunk the blood of most of them**....

The **death penalty is still on the Statute Books in most States in Australia**. Though it appears that opposition to it is growing quickly.

Migrants keep coming, but pay a great price. Maira Kalmius, a seven-year-old Latvian, is the 50,000th **European** migrant welcomed to Australia. Her ship was boarded at Newcastle, and she consented to receiving a publicity kiss from Migration Minister Arthur Calwell.....

One Letter-writer said she would **rather have gone back to Latvia** than accept that kiss....

Three days later, the same Minister will give a similar welcome in Melbourne to **the 100,000th migrant from Britain**. The young girl recipient of the kiss will have her parents and two brothers there to maintain propriety if the 6-year-old girl gets carried away....

You can see that **our post-War migration programme is in full swing.**

Field Marshall Fritz Manstein was being tried as a war criminal. He had been a Nazi, and was **accused of the murder of 100,000 Jews in the Crimea, and 16 other war crimes in Poland....**

This serves as a reminder that **War Trials against Nazi and Japanese alleged criminals were still being vigorously prosecuted.** In most cases, a guilty verdict, and execution, followed.

Police in Sydney have renewed their **raids on baccarat schools all over the city.** Flying squads are swooping on sheds, and flats, and tin huts, and swanky apartments after midnight in a bid to stamp out this **"moral turpitude and sinful behaviour"**....

At each location, a dozen men are taken to the local police stations. They are fined, and released, and **the baccarat school pays their fines**, and sets a new venue for the coming night's play. **The police intervention makes no dent in the appetite for gambling**, but does give the school some good advertising.

MEMORIES OF THE COAL STRIKE

My father was a coalminer, and about the same age as Chifley. For decades, he supported everything Chifley did. He simply hated the capitalists, and the mine-managers and owners, because, he said, they were mercilessly exploiting the miners day in and day out until they died. Somehow, Labor was reputed to have some magic wand to wave against this, so his support for that party was total and totally blind.

When the troops were brought into Abermain, one Company of about forty soldiers was unloaded at one end of the town, at Chinaman's Hollow, and then it marched in ranks of three through the two miles of town. When some children hid under the town bridge and threw stones at them, the Captain in charge stopped the march, and fixed bayonets. Then pranced up and down across the bridge a few times, looking over the edge. He must have decided that there were enough of the enemy camouflaged there to warrant further action, because he then sent a detail of one corporal and three privates down to capture the miscreants.

When they got there, they found three 13-year-old boys hiding in the rushes, and these boys seemed a little un-nerved to have 303-rifles, complete with bayonets, pushed in their faces. Meanwhile the news that this military operation was in progress had spread to the adjacent small shopping centre and a crowd of parents had gathered. They started abusing and cat-calling the Captain commanding, and generally indicated quite a degree of hostility to our own troops engaged in this Abermain Campaign.

Under the bridge, the corporal was a bit smarter than his superior. He told the lads to stay still, and not to try to "piss off". Then he took the detail and reported to the Officer that the perpetrators had fled. Whereupon, the whole squad was marched to the far edge of town, to pit property, and were not seen in town again.

It was a silly display of power by a silly young man. Other towns did not have this type of display, and the soldiers were received with good humour, and quite enjoyed their stay. The three lads were treated as heroes, but they admitted to being a bit scared at the sight of 14-inches of cold steel. The persons most shaken by the incident were probably the detail who went to seek the boys, and probably did not relish the idea of garroting a swarming hoard of three Australian school children.

My father's world fell apart. He rarely swore, or blasphemed, but now he did them both with much aplomb. His most telling remark was that "for years we have been frightened of the Japs invading us and now it's not the Japs, it's the Australians doing it." He managed to squeeze in a few extra words that, even today, are not fit to print.

Needless to say, the gaoling of the union leaders, and the stopping of strike pay, devastated him. And to cut this story short, he was one of **the hundreds of thousands of unionists who swore that Chifley was a capitalist mongrel**, and come what may, would never ever get his vote again.

Another interesting aspect of this was the arrival, a few days later, of a dozen policemen to the town. These young constables mixed in easily with the townsfolk. They stayed for over a week, and were domiciled in the bottom pub. It was a time of six-o'clock closing, so that when the beer went off about ten o'clock, they would come out in pairs, and walk the streets shining their light in our faces, and saying things like "you must be cold; would you like to borrow my jumper."

During the strike, the Strike Committee (one in every town) organised three evening concerts a week, on alternate nights, to keep up the morale of the workers. Anyone who could even whistle was encouraged to perform. Two of the invading policemen entered the Ambulance Hall one night, after ten o'clock of course, and were prevailed on to sing *The Beau Gendarmes*. They repeated this each evening, and when they left a week later, a few of the young ladies were moved to cry openly. They thought they would miss their singing.

Anyway, the intervention of the troops was really a joke. These poor lads were supposedly sent up to work in the open cuts. In those days, there were virtually no open cuts in the Northern NSW fields, and so some of the foolhardy ones volunteered, and were sent into the tunnel of the abandoned **underground mine**, Abermain No.1. They got lost immediately, and were rescued a day later by the Mines Rescue Squad, who, I am happy to say, knew how to go slowly when it seemed proper. I believe that not one shovelful of coal was actually produced from Abermain.

The Strike Committee was active on another front. It had to keep the workers simmering with resentment, and willing to keep up the fight. So, they maintained their own and the English tradition of having weekly torchlit marches through the town to a meeting place. The torches of course were not the electrical ones of the modern day variety, but long rags soaked in kerosene, and wound round six-foot sticks. The whole procession paraded the full length of the town, out to Chinaman's Hollow, where a group of rabble-rousing Reds fired them up for another week, ready for the barricades perhaps. It was spectacular stuff; three hundred men and children walking and growling through the cold winter night, with their torches raised above their heads, and joined at the Hollow by another three hundred from Weston. Along the way, old Welsh mining songs were sung by the marchers, and the dismal messages of oppression got them into the right mood. At the ground, there were no loud-speakers or even semaphores, so it was impossible to hear anyone over the hustle and bustle of the crowd. Still shouts of support came from everywhere.

Then the miners walked home, before their torches ran out of kero. If next day had been a working day, in the middle of winter, they would have been at pit top half an hour before sun-up, and would have stayed down till 90 minutes after sundown. Then for a cold shower at the pit head, in bathrooms with 100 other filthy men. Then home to tea and bed and, normally, safely tucked in by 8 o'clock. Then up on the Saturday morning for only a half shift. And all they had to risk was death and mutilation on a dozen levels.

It was this death and mutilation that was always at the forefront of their minds. Looking back, I ask myself why did they not just leave the industry? After all, there were now plenty of other jobs going. Why not take one of them, even if it meant moving out of the coal-fields?

I can think of a few reasons. Firstly, they had homes and friends and relatives right there. In those days, people were not nearly as mobile as they are now, and to go out of the insular and closed society of the mines to another spot meant a big change. Then there were job skills. Miners learned particular skills that did not transfer to other jobs. How many employers want a man who can shovel twenty tons of coal into a head-high skip six days a week? Not many, I can tell you.

On top of that, they had no capital. It takes money to pack up and leave, and miners did not have that. Finally, there was the fact that, if they had spent ten years down the mine, they were already significantly dusted, so that if there was any sort of fitness test for a new job, they were absolutely doomed to fail.

What about my father. Why did he not leave? Well, he tried to, at age 46. He applied for a position in a "dust-free pit" that was mooted to open at Camden. He was sent for a medical and he failed because they found he was two-thirds dusted. He was terminated the day the results were sent through.

Let me just add that being a labourer in those days, whether miner, or iron-worker, or road-worker, was tough. Every one of these you talk to says the same thing: thank God things have got so much better.

MRS O'KEEFE BACK IN THE NEWS

Mr Calwell had been hurt by the High Court decision on Mrs O'Keefe. But, not at all daunted, he was soon back into the fray. One correspondent said he had retired to lick his wounds, but found them to be not bleeding, because he had no heart.

So in mid-June he was back in Parliament with two Bills to cover the loopholes that had allowed O'Keefe and a handful of others to stay here. The second of these was to give him power over aliens who had come to Australia during the War, and were at present protected from him. This included Mrs O'Keefe.

The *SMH* saw dangers in these Bills. It regretted the fact that the Government had approved these Bills, because it **drew attention to the fact that it was its accepted policy that we should be so hard-hearted in our administration of the Acts.** There were some 800 affected remaining refugees here, out of a total of 6,000 Asians allowed entry during the War. Mr Calwell, the *SMH* continues, apparently assumes that this small rump could become somehow dangerous within a population of seven million people.

The proposals were too sweeping. Mr Calwell simply had to certify a person as being within the scope of the Act, and he would be so treated. It would mean, for example, that they could be forced to take **the dreaded language test**.

Mr Calwell, during the debate, also pointed to several of the features of our immigration policy. The best way we could help Asia was to admit students, and give them access to our technological information, and we were doing that now. He put forward the view that, even if we took in a small quota of Asian immigrants, this would be a minute drop in the bucket for these emigrant countries, and make no difference at all. He made the point that if migrants had come here during the War, and it was only because of the War that they got in, then **surely after the War was over, they should now leave**.

Despite these interesting arguments, the *SMH* found against Calwell. It concluded that the issue was not, and never was, issues surrounding the White Australia Policy It is whether "Australia's reputation, and the decent intentions of her ordinary citizens, are faithfully served by a Minister's ignoble pursuit of a few unhappy individuals."

The Australian Council of Churches agreed. It send a telegram to Bob Menzies during the debate, asking him to seek amendments that would ensure that certification decisions were made by an independent committee, and not by Mr Calwell and his Departmental officials.

The Bill was read a second time and debate was adjourned. The Government had the numbers, and so it was certain to be passed soon. **Where did that leave Mrs O'Keefe?** I will tell you after the break.

BLACK AND WHITE AREN'T MIXING

The 24-year-old white Ruth Williams from Blackheath in England married a black African studying at Oxford. He was the *heir apparent* to the throne of Bechuanaland, a large tribe in South Africa.

There was great resistance in the tribe, and from most blacks in South Africa, to the imposition of a white queen. Malan,

Prime Minister of SA, said the possibility was nauseating, and other people of prominence thought it was various shades of disastrous. The Prince was forced to abdicate, and was exiled.

This episode shows the racial hatreds that were common in many countries. It wasn't just in South Africa: it was in most former colonies where the white man had reigned supreme. And indeed in the Western World....

Post Script. The couple returned to Bechuanaland in 1956, and he eventually won the Presidency of the new State on four occasions. She flourished through this, and was eventually honoured and made a British Dame.

The story of the couple was made into the British film *A Marriage of Inconvenience* in 1990. The screamer used for it was *A white woman dares to marry a black man.*

Car-minders come to Sydney. The European tradition of having someone mind your car may be coming to Sydney. So says the Secretary of the NRMA. These self-appointed persons were now working in an area of Sydney, and demanding payment from persons who parked there. This is a custom in many parts of Europe and there most such attendants wore peaked hats with braid on, and also sometimes the jackets of gaudy military uniforms.

The motorist might consider that because these attendants are unlicensed, and they do nothing to protect cars, they can be ignored. But this is not true. If you do not contribute on the first occasion, you might find on return to your car that the tyres are flat.   On the second occasion, they might be slashed.

THE PRIVY COUNCIL

Going back a few years, **in 1947 Chifley had passed legislation to nationalise all banking in Australia**, so that **every person and business would be forced to bank with the Commonwealth only**. There was enormous resistance to Chifley on this (see my 1947 and 1948 books), and it was defeated in the Australian High Court. So Chifley appealed to the Privy Council in London, and hoped to get it validated there.

Now, back to 1949, it was at last announced that **his proposals were not valid**. The Act was not legal, and **his hopes of nationalisation were doomed**.

This meant that, for the time being, Chifley would not press on with alternative legislation to achieve his purposes, but all observers were certain that he would do just that, if he won the next election. The failure of the appeal was, according to Menzies, a bitter pill that was made difficult to swallow because **Chifley had been an advocate of regulation and nationalisation for twenty years**. But, for the time being, it was goodbye to any move on the banks.

THE LOVELY PRINCESS MARGARET

Meanwhile, life in England had gone on as if there had been no coal strike here. Funny that. Princess Margaret was now starting to make the headlines, as she got towards what people thought was *that age*. News sources say that the King has given her permission to announce her engagement on her 20th birthday, if she so wishes. But the reports also say that, while she does have many friends, "not even the most alert American keyhole peeper claims to have seen her holding hands with any one of them." One paper goes further and implies she is a bit wild. She had been seen drinking pink champagne in a West End nightclub, and had displayed her pretty legs in a Can Can at a private party.

MEANWHILE, SOME TRIVIA

Nothing so salubrious was happening back in Australia, though the Philippines' Consul General was having fun. He was about to return home, and his last few months had been plagued by disputes with Calwell over the deportation of his nationals. Recently, his wife had borne a son. He said that the boy would be named Arthur, after Mr Calwell, in appreciation of all that the latter had done for him. "He added a laugh that seemed to be tinged with irony. No, no, he said, this is not a joke. At least, **my son** is not the joke."

He went on to lament the fact that **the Immigration Department had required a taxation clearance for his four-week old baby**. Given that members of the Diplomatic Corps do not pay tax, and do not need taxation clearances, he found this odd.

SEPTEMBER NEWS ITEMS

A polio epidemic is taking its toll right across this nation. For example, in Victoria, kindergartens and crèches have been closed till further notice. Attendance at schools has been made voluntary, and numbers have dropped by 20 per cent, and are falling every day....

The idea is to stop the dread disease from spreading by avoiding crowds. But this is a bit of a gamble since no one is certain how the disease spreads....

469 cases have been reported in Victoria alone, and these include 31 deaths.

Tokyo Rose was the name given to a Japanese-American girl who **broadcast demoralising messages to Allied troops in the Pacific and Asia during the War**. Her daily radio show kept up the constant message that Japan was winning the War, that **the girlfriends of our soldiers were being unfaithful**, and that American "moms" had already forgotten their sons....

She was found guilty, but acquitted in 1956, and received a Presidential pardon in 1976. She got a better deal than **the British traitor Lord Haw Haw**, who made similar broadcasts from Germany into Britain. **He was executed in 1946.**

The visiting British Bishop of Chichester is a brave man. He said in Sydney that many former Nazis, because of their calibre, energy and genius, would make good migrants. That is, good migrants to Australia. His views in Australia were not well received.

In 1949, there were 395 known drug addicts in Britain. Of these, 198 were men, and 197 were women....

What do you think the numbers would be now?

King George VI has given orders that the Queen be appointed **Commander-in-Chief** of the Bedfordshire and Hertfordshire Regiment.

A woman living in Redfern, a Sydney suburb, found a **25-pound unexploded bomb** under the stairs leading to her bedroom. It had a live detonator and would have exploded if manhandled. She had lived in the house for only a few months, and this was the first time she had looked under the stairs. Police have no information on who left it there, and indicate that they will not be searching for the villain, because there **are no regulations that forbid leaving a bomb in a suburban home**.

Still in Redfern, **forty children were rushed to hospital violently ill**. A lorry had been parked outside a store, and a mob of children grabbed hold of some big bags of **tung oil nuts**, raced round the corner and banged them with rocks until they broke open. **They ate them, and suffered severe gastroenteritis....**

Some other miscreants took nuts home, and their parents ate them, and were soon "writhing in pain and foaming at the mouth." Everyone recovered after a few hours....

Of course, **my readers all know all about tung oil nuts**, so I don't need to describe them to you. I will just say that they are normally used in making varnishes, and - even today - no diets recommend them for eating.

A BOXING TRAGEDY

News item, Sydney Stadium. Police say they will not lay any charges against Jack Hassan, following the death of boxer Archie Kemp last month. The two fighters had battled for the Australian Lightweight Title, and Kemp was knocked out in the 11th round. He died without regaining consciousness.

Kemp was a bit groggy before the start of the round, but the referee Joe Wallis thought he was fit to continue. Hassan said that during the round it seemed that Kemp was no longer up to it, and so he paused his attacks, but had to go on when the fight was not stopped.

Letters, P Revell. The fatality at the Sydney Stadium should cause all right-thinking people to raise a protest against the inhuman practice called boxing, where people are permitted by law to injure and sometimes to slay and maim their fellow men.

We point a finger of scorn at nations where bullfighting is permitted; and we have cruelty-to-animals laws on our Statute Books; yet we allow humans to batter humans, then add insult to injury by calling the practice a "noble art".

Letters, D Smith. It is 1500 years since Telemachus, in the act of making a public protest against gladiatorial combats, was stoned to death by an infuriated Roman mob. This week, in Sydney, a man was killed under circumstances which might well cause this ancient hero to turn in his grave.

Anybody with even a rudimentary knowledge of the anatomy of the head and neck knows that boxing involves a very real and serious danger to the life and physical and mental health of the fighter. It is common knowledge that few professional fighters end their careers without serious injury, and that they are often unfit for any further work.

No other profession would tolerate the danger and physical suffering which are the common lot of the "pro". It cannot be fairly argued that these men earn large rewards, for no amount of money can compensate them for loss of health. It must also be remembered that most of them, preliminary fighters, are paid a miserable pittance.

We must not look to fight promoters to remedy this state of affairs. Their primary consideration is making money, and they have always been notorious for their callous disregard for the welfare of the men who make their fortunes for them. It is clearly the duty of the Government either to prohibit professional fighting as it now exists, or immediately take steps to ensure that it is conducted with humaneness. Expert physicians should be consulted, and their advice taken.

Australia has led the world in many reforms: here is her chance to point the way again.

Letters, E Pockley. Is it not possible to have gloves so padded that fatal results are impossible, and decisions awarded on points?

There might be arguments on points decisions as opposed to the knockout, but there would be fewer brutal and brutalising spectacles.

Letters, G Dupain. The death of Archie Kemp in the boxing ring raises real doubts as to the value of this sport in general.

Clinical research has shown it to be dangerous. Repeated blows to face, chin, head, and neck make brain injury inevitable, and it must be realised that the recuperative powers of brain tissue are much less than those of muscle, bone, and joint tissue.

There is only one answer to the present system, and that is to inaugurate some kind of control through a Boxing Commission.

Comment. These writers and others show a great deal of concern for the well-being of the young fighters. Many writers would like to ban fighting altogether. The trouble with this is that **while poverty exists** – and it always will – so too will the desire of some ambitious youngsters **to escape from poverty**. There are not too many ways to do that. Getting a steady job or studying hard might appeal to some, but there is a percentage that simply cannot do this.

Many of them, for example, do not have the grey matter to make it through study. Whether we like it or not, there will always be a supply of young men who want to get rich quickly, and who will take the risk of doing something like boxing. Another more sophisticated group who do the same thing, without the risk to life and limb, are those who walk greyhounds every day. And even more sophisticated, and this time with money to start, are the owners and trainers of race horses. **My point is that for the very poor, take away boxing, and another extreme sport will take its place.**

The best thing I can offer for boxing is that since the time of Hassan and Kemp, fighters have many fewer contests than they did then, and gloves have been modified. A good fighter then would have as many as twelve contests a year. Nowadays, many would scarcely have four.

TAKE IT EASY

Over the last few Chapters,we have set a busy tempo, and serious matters have dominated. For the rest of this Chapter, I will slow things down a bit, and look at a range of Letters, that reflect somewhat lesser concerns. Though the writers would not necessarily agree with that.

Sterilisation. Letters, Disgusted. I read with disgust Bishop Barnes' rabid speech in which he advocates **sterilisation** and, if necessary, **euthanasia for the unfit and decrepit**.

There seems to be little difference between what Dr Barnes proposes and what Hitler practised. If I had a malformed child, that child would have a right to life, which no State, whether it be Hitler's Germany, Stalin's Russia, or Barnes' Britain, has the right to take from him.

Letters, Scientist. Your writer "Disgusted" should be reminded that unless the Democracies take steps to ensure that habitual criminals, mental defectives, and those whose off-spring would become social menaces are prevented from propagating their kind, they will eventually become nations of high-grade morons.

Bishop Barnes is to be congratulated on his courage in discussing a subject of the utmost importance to the future of the British race.

A majority of the States of the United States of America now have laws providing for the sterilisation of specified types of persons whose reproduction would jeopardise social conditions; would complicate the problems of government; and add greatly to the tax burdens of the rest of the citizenry. **Over 14 other countries have passed sterilisation laws.**

It is obvious that the social burden of taking care of an increasing proportion of people who are helpless becomes either intolerable or impossible.

Sterilisation permits an afflicted individual much more freedom; permits him to marry; permits him to live as nearly normal a life as is consistent with the social welfare.

Perhaps your correspondent can suggest an alternative method for protecting the quality of our citizenry. It is not generally appreciated that upon this quality depends the continuance of our democratic way of life.

Death penalty. The Editor of the *SMH* got into this social-conscience mode.

He wrote that in NSW there were over a dozen crimes for which the death penalty was **prescribed**. That is, if the person is found guilty, the death penalty must be given. He argued that the number should be cut down to only two, that is, murder and treason. This would keep it in line with Victoria and "practically the whole of the civilised world".

For two and a half years, the State Attorney General has told us that an amending Bill can be presented at a moment's notice, but it has not been forthcoming. In the meantime, **juries are being deterred from giving guilty verdicts**, because they know a death sentence will be pronounced if they do.

Parking meters. Letters, A Leventhal. All the proposals to **install parking meters in the city** must surely be another method to obtain further revenue from the already overtaxed motorist.

The present parking regulations were put into force to avoid congestion in our crowded streets and would not be improved by the installation of meters. The parking police would still have to be employed to check the meters in order to "book" vehicles which had overstayed the time.

Further, the driver who stops for a few minutes must pay the fee for the whole period and the next user of the space would be entitled to the balance of the period free.

Lastly, would purely commercial vehicles be expected to pay a fee for each of the dozens of times they stop in their rounds of the city or would only certain types of road users be imposed upon?

Letters, SECOND MOTORIST. During a recent visit to America, where I travelled many thousands of miles, I found the network of parking meters which disfigure the streets in city and hamlet alike, to be one of the most vicious and widespread rackets in the country.

The meters solved no parking problems, but certainly filled the coffers of the city fathers. We can only blame ourselves if we permit the introduction of so execrable an idea which has achieved little abroad and will do less here.

The Sydney City Council explained its move to introduce meters. First, it said, let us assure you that they were **not meant to be permanent**. They are just a "temporary measure". They are designed to foster a greater turnover in parking spaces. In fact, "only businessmen who can afford it" will be able to park unmoved all day. These meters will stop "some selfish people parking all day, while others go without".

The *SMH* bemoans the fact that the meters will not add one yard to the parking spaces available. It points out that the Council had considered the building of an underground station, but had rejected it after years of debate. Collecting more money from motorists is not the solution. What is the solution is to provide more spaces any way possible.

Public-address systems. A brief news item in the *Herald* stirred some hidden passions.

Letters, R Johnson. I was horrified to read in the "Herald" that a public-address system is installed in the new Riverina Express.

This ubiquitous nuisance is apparently to invade the privacy of our carriages with details of places of interest and time-tables. No longer may we doze or read as we wish – all will be compelled to look right, look left, or look smart at the bidding of some hidden inquisitor.

There is, perhaps, a case for the public-address system at railway stations, but to spread the agony is both unnecessary and unkind.

Those who wish to enjoy the scenery do so without instructions; those who pass their time otherwise do not want to be disturbed.

Letters, A Williams. The complaint at the installation of the public address system on the Riverina Express assumes that it is of the type one hears at political meetings or from the top of police cars, strident and nerve-racking.

In fact, it is well modulated, clear, and of no more intensity than the tone employed in conversation, and I shall be greatly disturbed to discover that the system is used for other than calls to the dining-car and warnings of the approach of set-down points.

It may not be long before a radio-telephone is installed on our long-distance expresses. Imagine your correspondent being paged throughout the train, whilst his caller fumed at the delay and expense. This state of affairs is obviated by pressing a switch and notifying the called party, preferably in dulcet tones.

Such things are part of the traveller's daily experience overseas, and it irks me to find the parochial view expressed when modern, labour-saving and efficient schemes are introduced.

Letters, G Mathers, St. James' Church, Sydney. May I echo the sentiments of R Johnson with regard to the menace known as the public address system? Noise is a big enough problem without adding to it unnecessarily.

Perhaps the Minister for Health or the Master in Lunacy, or some other person whose office brings him into touch with some of the results of noise operating on the human nervous system would be good enough to take up the cudgels on behalf of residents of the Rushcutters Bay area.

For some time now, these unfortunate people have been compelled to endure the atmospheric detonations occasioned by the lusty yells of athletics, footballers, and their numerous and vociferous friends on week-ends. The Sunday afternoon nap is no more! But is it necessary to blast our ear-drums with the magnified distortions of this wretched instrument, as was the case last Saturday afternoon and on other occasions?

Letters, J Garven. The deaf or only partially deaf, constitute a fairly large percentage of our population, and since 1928, when the talkies replaced the silent pictures, they have been deprived of that form of relaxation and enjoyment.

There can be no doubt that if a certain percentage of the **silent films** were shown on the screen, or better still, if some theatres in our cities and larger towns were entirely devoted to them, **they would be extremely well patronised**. Patrons would include a large number of people who remember the old-time silent pictures as vastly superior to the present-day talkies. In those days many people who had cultivated tastes experienced the pleasure of attending such outstanding productions as "The Ten Commandments", "The Four Horsemen of the Apocalypse", "Annie Laure", and similar greats.

There was a slower tempo in the delivery of these pictures than in the talkies, and it therefore gave aged people in particular more time to thoroughly absorb and understand any play or subject that was screened.

Then again, more and different passions were stirred, this time by a simple Letter.

Letters, Docet. I am neither a "teetotaler" nor "wowser", but if you can tell me of anything that is more objectionable than a drunken or half-drunken person on a passenger train I have yet to find it.

The Minister for Transport, Mr O'Sullivan, says he has seen people rush madly down a platform and have three or four drinks before it is time to go, and in this way make themselves objectionable.

Obviously the Minister does not travel much on our passenger trains. The drinks obtained at the railway refreshment rooms are so small and the time so limited on these trains that drink obtained is harmless. **Bars on trains** would be a different matter altogether.

Letters, E Sheldon. Perhaps the Commissioner for Railways, Mr Garside, is right in refusing to allow liquor on his new air-conditioned trains.

In Europe, civilised drinking is the custom of the people, so this controversy would not have arisen. Liquor on European trains is as automatic as the wheels on which they run. In New South Wales we are not educated up to these refinements. We are accustomed to the six o'clock hog swill habit. Drink as much as you can whilst the going is good.

A de luxe train in Europe on which only milk and lemonade were served with meals would be an insult to the passengers.

Letters, O Piggott, Secretary, NSW Temperance Alliance. The reported remarks of the Minister for Transport, Mr O'Sullivan, regarding the sale of liquor on the Riverina Express indicate that the Minister has a very short memory.

In 1942 a liquor bar was opened on the Riverina Express and as a result many travellers complained of the trouble caused by drunken individuals. The first day the bar was opened there was a minor riot on the train. My organisation protested to Mr O'Sullivan, with the result that the Commissioner closed the bar.

The present Commissioner, with a full knowledge of these facts, has very wisely in the interests of the travelling public banned the sale of liquor on the train. It would be a backward step to do otherwise.

Letters, G Charles. The Australian public have only themselves to blame for lack of amenities on public transport.

Toilet conveniences provided for general comfort are usually left in a disgusting condition; rubbish left anywhere but in receptacles provided. Railway property, such as glasses and water bottles are merely considered as good marks for souvenir-hunters. Those who transform carriages into "self-service restaurants" think nothing of leaving food scraps under the seat, to the intense discomfort of other travellers, especially on long-distance lines.

If liquor is provided, the railway employees would have to contend with the disgusting drinker who does not know how much is enough. Such people only represent a hazard to public convenience and a danger to themselves and other travellers.

Let the Australian public prove they can use such normal amenities in a civilised manner and then they will get more and more. At present it seems that providing even comfortable sitting accommodation is a waste of public money.

OCTOBER NEWS ITEMS

Industrial trouble in the US. A nation-wide steel strike of 500,000 workers is due to start at midnight. 480,000 miners have been out on strike for 12 days. Violence has broken out at some pits where **dynamite** was used to destroy above-ground materials, **a two-hour gun battle** was fought at another.

A number of **scabs** are working under police guards. At one pit, **helicopters** were used by police to break up miners on a picket-line. The police dropped **tear-gas bombs** on to the strikers.

Comment. Our own recent miners' strike seems mild by comparison.

Bright sparks. In the inner-city Sydney suburb of Erskinville, a motorist was in his dark garage taking petrol from his 44-gallon drum reservoir to put into his car. He could not see if the bucket he was using was full, **so he lit a match to see**. An explosion occurred, and a Chinese restaurant, a pub, and two adjacent houses were damaged. No one was hurt. He explained "It was only a **wax** match. **They're really small.**"

Here's one for the oldies. Do you remember a song entitled *If You Were the Only Girl in the World*? Well, sorry to say, the French composer Wally Redstane died in Sydney. He came to Australia in 1921, and worked at the ABC since then. He was paid five guineas for the sentimental song.

An oil geologist working near Roma in Queensland has found 40 feet of a spinal **skeleton of a dinosaur....**

The beast would have been over 100 foot long. This unusual find in Australia stirred up arguments about **the evolution of mankind**. There were many people who claimed that **God had created the world**, while just as many claimed that the **world and its creatures had evolved over time....**

Comment. Seventy years later, the Creationists are in retreat, though not completely vanquished by any means. I bet that every reader knows someone who believes still **that Adam and Eve indeed started the human race**.

The public was starting to **fear the atom bomb** might be used to bomb the nation. No one was clear just where the threat would come from, or why, but fear was evident everywhere. The newspapers were very keen to keep the fear as high as possible because it was good for sales....

Last Sunday, the *SMH* published a 16-page Supplement that talked about the making of bombs, and **how to react when one was exploded near you**. It was a big success, so now the *SMH* is selling the Supplement at three pence a copy, post free....

This was just the beginning. For the next 20 years, the **world lived in the shadow of the Bomb**. Many children born in the Fifties, when saying their evening prayers, asked to be spared if an attack came before morning. **But there were others**, including myself, who said that it was all scare-mongering, we said. All paper-talk....

These latter people were right - so far.

FREE MEDICINE

Chifley had long been intent on **forcing doctors to participate** in his scheme to **make some medicines free to most of the population** (see my 1948 book). By this time, **his scheme had been placed before the High Court and rejected**. Chifley had had a number of ideas, **all based on nationalisation or socialism** that had ended up before the Court, or in a referendum. **In every case, he was rebuffed.**

Here is just one person's opinion of the issue involved.

Letters, F Coss. Some South Coast miners have struck as a protest against the decision of the High Court in the case of the Pharmaceutical Benefits Act. The miners complain that the High Court rejected "progressive legislation" and upheld "anti-working class legislation".

In its judgment the High Court stated that, as the Act would impose a form of civil conscription upon members of the medical profession, it was invalid. No doubt the miners would be the first to oppose most strenuously any attempt to impose a form of civil conscription upon them as a means of increasing coal production.

In basing its judgment upon the fact that the Act would involve an infringement of the civil liberties of a group of people, the High Court has again shown that it is the guardian of our freedom – the freedom not only of the medical profession, but also of the miners.

Any Act which threatens to interfere with our civil liberties could well be described as "anti-working class legislation" because the working class would be most affected by it. Irrespective of our political beliefs, we should all view this decision with the greatest satisfaction.

But despite such issues, and despite the constant rejection by all concerned, **Chifley persisted with his socialism plans**. Immediately after this latest rejection by the High Court, he started to talk about drafting new legislation that would get his scheme through. The question is, **why did he persist?** I would have thought that any Prime Minister who **was so constantly rejected** would have dropped his plans, and gone down a different road. But he did not.

Perhaps you could put it down to stubbornness, or to ego. There are a lot of people who, having made their decisions public, will not change even if later they are clearly wrong. Perhaps you can say that he had a vision and was convinced it was right for the people. And then go on to say that he was more noble than other politicians who change their spots when looking down an electoral gun-barrel. I am not sure about that one; in fact, I see lots to suggest he was just as quick to change horses as anyone else when confronted by adversity.

But perhaps we should now see it from the perspective of seventy years ago. At this stage, in 2019, at election time we are faced almost daily with all sorts of polls that tell politicians how they are going and what elements of policy are profitable. Could it be that back in Chifley's day, when there were none of these polls, he did not get that information, and had to gauge opinion from the people he spoke to? And that he thus got the impression that the people loved him and considered him the sage custodian of their fortunes? It would explain why **he just ran on his record, and put forward no new policies or visions**. Maybe it is the right reason. Or maybe it's the combination of ten reasons. Anyway, I suggest you think about it.

PETROL RATIONING

Petrol is the burning issue. Back in June, I left you with Ben Chifley saying that he would not increase petrol supplies above the current levels. And the State Premiers were ever so keen not to cop the blame for introducing rationing to their States. **When the High Court declared that rationing was illegal**, there had been a moment of joy, because motorists had thought that this meant abundant supplies of petrol for them. Everyone had gone to the pumps and filled up, and if this meant that garages ran out of supplies earlier than usual that month, then it was no problem because they would soon be getting more. The canny ones, and there were plenty of these especially in the country, **took this brief moment of hope to fill up 44-gallon drums**, and any other canister they could lay their hands on. The dreaded, and illegal, practice of hoarding got a new life. We hear a lot about petrol hoarding, and the **city** motorist with his tin pot and his four or six gallons

But also of **the country regions**, where thousands of 44-gallon drums were stored since the lifting of rationing. Some country people have been openly boasting that they have enough petrol to last them for two years. Surely this type of hoarding needs looking into.

But all good things come to an end, they say. And certainly this did. Next month, there was just the same amount as in the previous months. **Chifley was sitting pat.** Australia needed dollars, he said, and we were not going to spend any more of them on junk like petrol. The Premiers started to realise that they had a real problem here, and that they would have to make some decisions pretty soon. The petrol was still being distributed but with no official system. If you were a relative or friend of the garage owner, you did well. So too did big customers. Anyone willing to pay a bit more got preference, and the fact that such trading was above the official price limit did not deter anyone for a minute.

At the other end, there were many persons with no special connections, and these were met with "sorry, mate, it's all gone". Let me just say that there were more reports of shortages among the general public than there ever had been under rationing.

The initial meetings between Premiers and the PM and government officials and company representatives went on and on. Chifley did not budge. He wanted to re-introduce official rationing, and so not a day went past without him hammering the needs we had for more dollars. At times, he even warned darkly that dollars were in such short supply that he might have to cut back even more on imports of petrol. But that did not actually occur; it was designed to push the Premiers into submission.

The Premiers were most reluctant to act. An editorial in the *SMH* said that they were unanimous in one respect – they were each waiting for some other State to be the first to agree to re-introduce rationing ; "the other fellow" must be saddled with as much of the odium as possible. If they were sure that Chifley would take the rap, they would let him have his way.

The editorial argued that the Victorian Holloway Government held the key to it all, that if it decided for rationing, the other States would fall in line. "But the Holloway Government suffers from a chronic incapacity to make up its collective mind on major issues, and it has been in an agony of indecision over petrol." Unfortunately, the agony continued. There was no end in sight.

There was always the hope that we could get petrol from non-dollar areas, like the Middle East and Russia. Other large nations did this and had an abundance of the fuel. Ampol Petroleum was very happy to arrange that, and applied for a licence to do so. Menzies and Fadden liked this idea, and gave it their full support. But, as the *SMH* commented, "The bare idea that such petrol might exist somewhere, and be procurable for Australian bowsers, has seemed to strike Mr Chifley and his colleagues as some sort of impropriety." They took the attitude that "such supplies did not exist, could not exist, and perhaps should not exist, and that was that."

Further, said Chifley, if such imports were possible, we still had to pay for them, and while the money would not come directly from our dollar purse, it would come from the sterling purse, and that would mean that we could buy less of sterling goods. But the final nail in Ampol's coffin came when it said that petrol from sterling sources would cost three pence a gallon more, and asked the Government to subsidise this. Mr Chifley, with whoops of delight no doubt, was able to refuse this request without criticism.

The stalemate continued until, in early October, the majority of the States (four, in fact) agreed to **the Commonwealth getting the power to ration petrol again**, for a period of about two years, and starting about mid-November. This decision was **not at all popular with the general public**. The *SMH* caught some of the discontent. "The prospect of a return to the form-filling, coupon-collecting, time-wasting routine of the post-war years is highly distasteful to everybody concerned, not excluding post-office staffs who will again have the issuing of tickets superimposed upon their ordinary duties."

The ration per motorist would be the same as before the interruption to the system. New coupons, now called tickets to fool people into thinking things were different, would be issued in time for November 15. The ration per motorist was quite small. If you had certain types of car, you got more. But typically if you had a middle-of-the-range car, you could expect to be able to drive about 200 miles per month. That is, for all you people who have accepted that the metric system is here to stay, about 320 Kms. That is about 10 Kms per day. You can see that petrol rationing really hurt.

Over the next month, the Government kept up the pressure. It announced in early November that motorists having more than 20 gallons of petrol at mid-night on Friday night must declare them to the Liquid Fire Control Authority. Further, no one with such stocks was now allowed to sell, dispose of, or use these stocks without permission. Rather generously, it added that petrol already in the tank would not be included in the 20 gallons. This was an attempt to get back at the people who had bought a few months earlier. But it did not specify penalties, and seemed to be heavy-handed and oppressive. The requirements were quietly modified, and re-modified, and the regulation died the ignoble death of all ignored regulations.

Mr Chifley had had his way. Rationing was back to where it had been, and our dollar pool was close to the brink. How long it might have lasted no one knows, but the States had given him a licence to continue for two years. That would have been a long time after the War ended. But, other events intervened, and so we won't worry ourselves about it.

DIRTY DANCING

The Synod of the Church of England in the Sydney diocese passed a motion deprecating "dances, card parties, and games of chance used in connection with Church activities."

The motion was sponsored by Rev K Shelley. He said that dancing came about among native peoples as an aid to sex stimulation, and it retains its original purpose among us to-day. Modern dancing has reached the lowest depths of licentiousness.

An American writer said that the waltz came about in the lowest of the low places in Vienna. It was not for a long time that it came into the social life of the city.

Mr T Faulkner, a converted dancing master, said the waltz was introduced by a licentious libertine named Gault in 1627, and he was guillotined for murder in 1632. A New

York Police Chief said that 75 per cent of fallen girls in New York were ruined by dancing.

A Roman Catholic Archbishop in New York said that 19 out of 20 of all fallen women confessed that they took their first downward step by dancing. "Must we parade **under the cloak of our Church** that which has its terrible origin in this way?"

An officer of the Salvation Army agreed. He said "No man should hold a woman in his arms unless he is married to her. We are totally opposed to dancing because it is worldly and leads to concupiscence."

The Presbyterian Church had a foot in both camps. The Moderator, Rev D Flockhart said "We do not approve on moral grounds. After all, dancing probably had its origins in pre-Christian religious rituals. We believe that the basic tenet of the Christian faith is: Be happy. Dancing can be included in that. The Church, however, does not approve of dancing as a means of raising money for Church purposes."

The Methodist Church said "definitely no dancing allowed on Church premises, although some of the more broadminded clergy tacitly approve young people's dances organised in secular halls."

The Catholic Church "regards dancing as a normal, healthy, and harmless recreation. Priests attend dances, although they do not, as a rule, dance. Catholic Youth Organisation groups in all parishes hold dances regularly. Even Cardinal Gilroy attends functions where dancing is held, and receives debutantes."

Reverend Kenneth Shelley was a thirty-five year old, non-smoking, non-drinking and non-dancing rector from Chatswood. He said that since his resolution was passed by the Synod, his letter-box has been crammed each morning with unsigned letters abusing him. He has been called a pussyfoot, a bigot, kill-joy, puritan and wowser.

He quoted from the Bible. "Whosoever shall offend one of these little ones that believe in life, it is better for him that a millstone were hanged about his neck and he were cast into the sea." He argued "How can the Church set an example to man if it panders to the imperfections in human nature."

A vivacious 25-year old, who loves dancing, offered to show him what dancing was all about. She would be happy to take him to a dance, and let him see for himself. She was sure he would enjoy himself. "I think there must be something lacking in his education. It would only take one dance to fix that."

A lady from Hunter's Hill also offered him a night out. At eighty-five years old, she would "gladly give him a dish of tea, and take him along to one of our dances". She, too, was sure he would enjoy himself.

A Miss Phyllis Bates, a ballroom-dancing instructor for twenty years, said that to talk about dancing as an aid to sex stimulus is absurd. "Young people don't need it. And older people would not go dancing to get it."

Letters, (Rev) H Reynolds. Rev Shelley's motion before Synod and his letter reflect a pharisaism explicitly condemned in the Gospels.

The statement, "The Church's task is to seek the lost sheep, not to amaze the goats", may appeal to Mr Shelley and those who think it as witty as he does, but others will regard it as being rooted in self-righteousness.

I am the rector of a parish that sponsors an occasional ball or dance. The most important of these each year is organised and run by a group of Anglican young people. I can assure Mr Shelley that I am proud of these young people and that they are among the most loyal members of their good Church.

I believe that dancing helps them, and others like them, to develop both social grace and dignity and physical self-control. Those who are morally harmed by dancing would surely come to grief in some other way if dances were forbidden them.

Letters, (Rev) O Abram, St Jude's Rectory, Randwick. The Rev Shelley's letter makes sad reading, coming from an Anglican, for it reveals a jaundiced Christian outlook.

By all means let "the Church possess clean hands, a pure heart, and an acute conscience", but surely that does not mean that she has to become so perfect that she can utter pharisaical denunciations against Christian people who like to express their joy in living and fellowship together by dancing, a friendly game of cards, and a lucky ticket even at a parish gathering.

Letters, Disturbed Youth. How much better for youth to meet at church halls, under the eye of the rector, to have their fun, instead of dancing in places such as night-clubs, which according to our seniors, cause many of us "to fall".

Youth with a Christian background does not dwell on the somewhat distasteful idea of sexual arousement. It is these sordid anticipations of our elders which put such ideas into our heads. We are aware that many evils have been associated with dancing, but these can be excluded by the truly Christian youth whose faith would be his guide through any such perils.

Letters, (Rev) Wm Rook. To healthy-minded youth, the substance of Mr Shelley's letter must be nauseating in the extreme.

I do not believe that our young people, despite what Mr Shelley says to the contrary, fall into the "pit of despair and degradation" through parish dances, any more than they may do so after attending a "squash" meeting or a church choir practice on Sunday.

The self-discipline that Mr Shelley speaks of will not come by legislation or prohibition, but by the Grace of God. There are countless numbers of our young people who have this Grace in their brains and yet dance and play cards to the glory of God.

Letters, B Baldwin. It is not surprising to read what the Rev Rook has to say about dancing and card-playing in churches and denouncing Mr Shelley, and others who are trying to uphold the standards of the church.

It is also no wonder that compromise in this has brought so many of our churches to the level they are in today, with empty pews and with lack of power, simply because many whose responsibility it is to "feed the flock" have lost the glow of their first Christian love and gone over to worldliness. Not only is this so in the Anglican Church, but even Methodists and Presbyterians and others are "experimenting" with this sort of thing with unfortunate results.

Until we get back to the fundamentals of our faith, the Church will continue to decline under the leadership of ministers who are not leading their people as they should. The function of the Church is to worship God, not to entertain.

Letters, OMR. I would go further than Brown and state that if Synod continues with their bigoted manner, there will be a third revolt in the life of the Church of England.

If Synod wishes to avert a division in the Church, they should not run away from their responsibility to our young folk, but should have a broader vision and use tolerance and discretion.

Comment. Not long after this conversation, **the Stomp craze swept the nation**. What would the above writers have to say about that?

NOVEMBER NEWS ITEMS

The nation was short of houses, desperately short. It also needed to develop many building lots. All governments were trying to provide these but with shortages of everything, the pace was slow. But the need was high, so **they found ways to ration the lots** as fast as they could....

One way was to develop an area of land into lots, and then **hold a lottery among the people who had put their names into the ha**t....

This month, NSW had a new development at East Killara, then on the fringe of Sydney. There were 19 lots, and 10 of them were reserved for ex-servicemen. **1,140 people put their name in for the draw.** You can see how many were disappointed. Finished **houses were also offered** in the same way.

The migrant ship *Anna Salen*, from Naples, arrived in Melbourne. Twenty four children were rushed to hospital suffering from **measles. Six had died en route. Another 36 had the disease**, but were not so severe, and were kept on board.

The UK Company, Courtalds, will open two factories in Australia. One will be at Newcastle in NSW. It will **produce rayon** that will be used in tyres and in fibres for clothing....

It is hoped that such **artificial fibres**, often coming as a by-product in the distillation of petroleum, **could become significant in producing clothing in the future**.

A crowd of 108,000 people went to Melbourne to see Foxzami win **the Cup** at 19 to 1.

In Newcastle, two members of the religious sect, the Exclusive Brethren, **refused to join the Electrical Trades Union on religious grounds.** They were sacked. The Industrial Commission ordered that they **be reinstated**. Now, the top Union body in NSW has decided that **the dismissals must be enforced**, and will not stand for men refusing to join a Union on religious grounds.

A 91-year-old man in Melbourne was **pouring kerosene** on his fire when it flared up and **set fire to his beard,** moustache, and clothing. He died from burns soon after.

Prince Charles is about to have his first birthday. The Master Bakers Association of Britain will present him with a great big cake to mark the occasion. They plan to put a quarter of a pint of rum into it "as is customary for a big cake". The Temperance Council of British Churches is very much against this. As one Member put it, "a whole generation of our youth could develop a craving for rum if this practice spread".

In these days before TV, **politicians stumped the nation as elections drew near**. With the Federal election due this month, Bob Menzies orated at Canterbury RSL to a hall full of supporters, and 1,000 listening outside to loud-speakers. The crowd inside had been screened so that there were virtually no interjections. He spoke for an hour and time ran out. He had to omit his thoughts on the White Australia Policy. "I was going like Foxzami at the end, so that I could get it all in."

THE PRICE IS NOT RIGHT

A few days ago, a Hurstville grocer was in no-man's-land because he sold tea at a price **below that specified** by the Commonwealth. He had been informed by the Commonwealth **Tea and Coffee Control Board** that, unless he put his prices up, he would be prosecuted. Butter and tea suppliers have since threatened him. He had 43 lines of groceries on specials, and he did not intend to be intimidated.

The **State Prices Commissioner** said he was quite right in doing this. He said that the prices specified were the maximum allowable, and if anyone wanted to charge less, it was up to him. He added that the grocer might have problems with other grocers in the area, but that was his own decision.

In the face of this conflicting advice, he persisted. The next day, his shop was full with customers all day. However, he was advised by his tea supplier that they would no longer supply him. Despite this, he re-ordered more tea that day. He also said he would take legal action if the tea was not forthcoming. The *SMH* found this very perplexing. It pointed out that it was true that the Commonwealth Tea Board said the maximum price must also be the minimum.

But it asks why this should be. Surely the objective of **price control is to keep prices down. Surely letting the price be reduced would achieve this.** It goes on to state that the Tea Board no longer has any say in the matter, because power to control prices has now passed to the States. The only consolation the Board can now have is that there will not be many grocers willing to cut their price.

As it turned out, the grocer need not have worried about his tea. It arrived the next day. One week later, he said that he might be able to reduce his prices on soap, jelly crystals, and baby powder. "There is a very big margin on soap. I am currently selling it at five pence a cake. I might be able to reduce it to four and a half pence a cake, and that would be a big saving."

This little episode is the beginning of price specials that are so common in shops nowadays. If you appreciate them, I think it would be nice to ring the grocer and say a few words of thanks. He was at Hurstville just on 70 years ago, and his name was Mr A Garton. I am sure he would appreciate your call.

THE SNOWY RIVER SCHEME

On a few occasions since September, Mr Chifley gave an outline of his plans to develop the Snowy River region in ways that "would develop the nation, and increase the population. It will also enlarge the foundations of our defensive strength, which in the troubled conditions of the world today, must rank among our foremost national objectives."

As the months progressed, he gave more and more details. Sixteen underground power stations, "hidden deep within the rugged fastnesses of the Snowy Mountains", and free from enemy attack, and not susceptible to the caprices of the coal miners, will provide the lifeblood for our factories and for our families.

By the start of October, all was ready, and after a well orchestrated promotional campaign, the Governor General, Bill McKell, former Premier of NSW, officially opened the scheme by pressing down on a plunger and thereby blowing up large sections of the neighbouring bushland. This act drew great applause from the assembled crowd of 4,000 people.

It also started a bushfire which a local journalist reported burned on a broad front well into November. Despite this, Mr Chifley was very enthusiastic that the seven dams would bring water to many people, and added that the scheme would provide the opportunity for important research in Canberra into atomic energy.

DECEMBER ELECTIONS COMING UP

The elections were due to be held on December 10th, and so the nation now went into election mode. Very early, there was a Letter published in the *SMH* that captured very well some of the finer elements of the democratic process.

Letters, E White. Soon we will be presented with the policy speeches of the main political parties.

No doubt these will vie with one another to give the most attractive conditions to every main voting element, such as the employees, farmers, and employers, etc., and at the same time attempt to avoid antagonising any of the diverse major pressure groups.

Is it too much to ask that these policy speeches, while promising to give the community all the material security and sound economic backing that the economy will stand, will at the same time give some assurance that the individual will not have his human freedom further curtailed, and that many of those freedoms which he has had filched from him on one pretext or another are restored to him?

Political parties are prone to treat their supporters as regimented sheep, a dumb driven mob, which willy nilly must and will support the party they normally give allegiance to. This is a mistaken idea; there are other considerations, vital to our civilisation, which far transcend mere material security and scientific and industrial progress.

The individual is now very largely at the mercy of mass control in one form or another, and in consequence his personality and thinking as an individual are suppressed to conform to mass objectives. This is highly dangerous to the future of humanity and civilisation, and while political parties may not regard any declarations of the subject as possessed of much vote-catching value, it is nevertheless of crucial importance and quite a few people realise that human freedom and individuality must be restored and sustained to the fullest extent.

Any party which comes out with a forthright and positive statement on the subject, and implements its declarations, will be deserving and will receive strong support for doing so.

Unfortunately, these truly fine sentiments hardly survived in the hurly burly of the real political world, and the protagonists were quickly at each other's throats.

THE ELECTION ISSUES

The nation will be going to the polls in a few weeks. They will be swayed by a number of issues that are important to them. Below I have given a summary of the major matters that the good people of this nation will take into their individual consideration.

White Australia Policy. Calwell had triumphed. He had fought and lost in the Courts, but had brought back legislation that let him throw out almost anyone he wanted, without interference from the independent committees that other nations used. He had thumbed his nose at Asia, and placed Australia right outside the spheres of Asian influence. In doing this, he had alienated about a billion Asians, (and me), but he was secure in the knowledge that none of them could get into the country to vote.

The thing that probably galled him the most was that he had not been able to get rid of Mrs O'Keefe and her tribe.

Free Medicine. The Government had lost its various Court cases, and vowed to resurrect the Bills next term. The BMA, representing the doctors, had gone quiet on this, near to the election. Clearly they thought that Chifley would lose the election and so the matter would go away in its present form and maybe not come back.

Banking. Would Chifley have another go? If you look around now, you can see from the number of banks that **he did not succeed in nationalising them**, so either he tried again and failed, or he did not try again. If you've followed my arguments throughout, you might be able to guess what happened, but I won't spoil it now for you.

Petrol. Chifley had got back his power to ration petrol. It was just another way in which **he felt that he knew best**, and that his Government should control the lives of citizens. He might have felt that he had won here, but the benefits to him were very dubious.

Unions and Communism. Chifley had had his win against the Communists in the coal strike, but he had lost a lot of support among the Unionists. In all, this win cost him many votes, and at this time, that is what mattered.

THE CAMPAIGNS

Chifley fired the first official shot of the campaign with his election speech. This was a curious event. It broke from normal precedent in that it was only 36 minutes long. This of course was a good thing, because an hour of his droning monotone would have been fatal.

But overall, in presentation, he lost out, because he pre-recorded his speech, and had it replayed over ABC radio some hours later. This seemed, to many, to be too impersonal. They liked the small blunders that speakers always made, and they liked the idea that the orator was talking directly to them. One commentator said Chifley had recorded it so that he could use it again at the next election. But in any case, the **presentation** of the speech drew much more attention than Labor wanted.

The **content** of Chifley's speech was very curious. He simply did not mention any of the issues I outlined above. The *SMH* editorial next day said "it was amazing for its omissions or evasions in relation to issues uppermost in the public mind." Petrol was not mentioned, Communism was mentioned only once in a different context, socialisation was not acknowledged. **On and on, he did not talk about the matters that were on everyone's lips.** But he did not come out with any alternatives, as he might. What he did do was ask the electors to "**judge us on our record** and on our ability to go on with the job of building Australia into the nation we want it to be."

He spent considerable time going back to issues that had been dead for twenty years:

So far as it is humanly possible, never again will the dole queue be seen in this country. Never again will competent workmen stand idle while limitless work remains to be done.

Never again will young men drift hopelessly from town to town, and from State to State, searching for the jobs which, in all this wide land, did not exist for them.

We can assure the Australian people that we will not allow an overseas slump to cripple our economic life, as happened in years gone by.

Mr Calwell joined in this denial of reality. He said "petrol, communism, socialisation, bank nationalisation are dead issues." The *SMH* commented, "It is pure coincidence that the subjects that have so suddenly and conveniently expired are those most embarrassing to the Government. If only, being dead, they would consent to lie down, how much easier for Chifley the electoral going would be."

Mr Evatt added his own twist. He said that the true issue was full employment. Again, I quote the *SMH*. It said that "As for full employment, we have not got it now. What we have is **over-full** employment combined with under-production and exorbitant costs." This statement was certainly true as far as employment was concerned, and no-one gave it a second's thought for years to come.

So, Labor bombed the election campaign. How did Menzies, and his merry men, fare? He was astute. He knew he was leading in the count, and that he simply had to avoid making mistakes. So, he hammered away on the issues that Chifley would not discuss, and kept them at the forefront of people's minds. The two changes he did promise were that **he would outlaw Communism, and that he would get rid of petrol rationing immediately**. How could he lose, I hear you say.

He was aided by his eloquence. Every time he spoke he came across as a charming, well-educated, intelligent, tough campaigner. He epitomised the type of Australian that would be perfect to represent this nation. The fact that he was as cunning and shifty as Chifley did not matter. He looked the goods.

The Liberals seemed to have an unlimited supply of money. Probably a lot of it came from the banks, which were still frightened of Chifley. Big business, keen to get rid of the Communists, was also a good contributor. The adverts that they ran in the papers were large, and they just kept coming. Similarly for radio coverage. In all, they blitzed it.

The Liberal ads had this simple theme. It said how Labor stands on its record. Then it laid out what that record was. On and on went the list of topics that Labor was attacked on. On coal, the punchline was "Chifley backed down to the Communists". On petrol "stubborn and wilful re-imposition of rationing". On corruption of Parliament "Chifley has supported biased Speakership". Each and every point that could be raised was raised, and some little slogan voiced. **There was often some truth in them, and others were scarcely credible.** In any case, they were everywhere you turned, simply expressed and very effective with the masses.

It was not only in the Press that the one-sided battle was waged. **The airwaves were full of plugs for the Liberals.** It wasn't just 30-second grabs with catchlines. It was 15- and 30-minute commentaries and satirical pieces and sometimes soap-operas with an obvious message. It had gone on for eighteen months, and now reached a crescendo. In all areas, Labor was completely out-gunned.

So, Labor limped into the last week of the campaign. Little did it know that **the wily old politician, Jack Lang, had set a trap for the Prime Minister**, and was waiting to spring it just before the election.

ELECTION FUNDING.

The huge difference between what the Parties had available to spend on the elections seems somehow unfair to me. I know that every party can spend as much as it can raise, and if it has a platform that is popular, then it will be able to raise more money.

Perhaps my misgivings come from that fact that the money for the Liberals was not coming so much from the man in the street, but rather big business. So that you could argue it was coming from a small coterie of rich people rather than small folk, and not at all from the grass-roots. But you need to balance that with the thought that the banks and businesses represent their shareholders, and employees and customers, and they should in turn have their say.

Having said that, I come back to the fact that the Liberals had so much money, and that Labor had so little. In our childhood dreams of democracy, it is easy to think that, at elections, if all other things are equal, then the winner will be the best men and the best policies. But in this election, all those other things were clearly not equal. One side was completely swamped. What does that do to our deep-seated concepts of democracy?

Of course, Labor brought some of this on itself. Normally, many businesses give donations to both political parties, though they will give more to the Liberals. But this time, why would any business give cash to a Government that might nationalise it at the drop of a hat? The answer is that it would not, and in fact, that they did not. Then there is the perennial problem that, in those years, all the major newspapers supported the Liberals. Labor had tried a few times to start its own paper, but without success. In this case, this deficiency just added to the blanket coverage against them.

If we look overseas, and if we look back and forward for a hundred years, this problem of unevenness is always apparent. There are always schemes to even it all out, and ideas that will make it fairer. But, over the years, the schemes seem in the longer run to end up with the same large imbalances.

So, when all is said and done, I look sad and shrug my shoulders, and say that our system of democracy might have some flaws in it, but it's the best we've got until something better comes along.

INDONESIA'S INDEPENDENCE

Indonesia's independence. On November 2nd, Dutch and Indonesian delegates announced a plan, thrashed out after ten weeks of negotiation, for establishing an independent State of Indonesia. It made the Netherlands and Indonesia partners in a Union, with the Dutch crown as the symbolic Head of State.

The negotiations agreed on Indonesia's financial and economic policy, with the recognition that the Dutch were an integral part of the future. But the Dutch Army would be withdrawn, though it would give training and advice. Large numbers of Dutch civil servants were encouraged to remain employed there and both nationalities were to be given equal opportunities in promotions. In New Guinea, no agreement had been reached, but it was accepted that they would return to discuss this in one year's time. **In short, it was a sensible agreement that was as good as you could get at the time.**

Post Script. On December 27, Queen Juliana of the Netherlands, in a simple ceremony, **closed out 340 years of Dutch colonial rule in the East Indies**. She described the transfer as "one of the most profound and moving events of this time".

Comment. In 1949, we knew very little about Indonesia. Now, at the time of writing these pages in 2018, we still know very little. **That seems to be a pity.** After all, they **are** our nearest neighbour, and have caused us no real concern in the past.

COMPLETE TRIVIA

Letters, W Harrison. It is time some action be taken by the citizens of Sydney to have the G.P.O. tower clock restored to its proper place.

The G.P.O. is an unsightly building without its clock – like a ship without its compass. Sydney impresses visitors as being the only big city in any country without a clock tower to its G.P.O.

Night trotting is here. Night trotting was introduced to Harold Park. For the first few months, attendances were reasonable but not exciting. But as it gained popularity, and as the nights warmed up, attendances were growing weekly. Over the next twenty years, these numbers grew, and by the 1970's, a good normal crowd was about 20,000, and much larger for Carnivals.

Hollywood. You will recall that in January there was a little controversy over whether Rita Hayworth should have an affair with a married man, the well-known play-boy, Prince Aly Khan.

We saw in April that she decided that Aly was the man for her, so she married him then. Now, she has gone one step further, and done her best for the Baby Boom, by giving birth to a bouncing baby boy.

DECEMBER NEWS ITEMS

The *Sydney Morning Herald* every day, at the top of Page One, advertised itself as "**The only 2-penny Daily Newspaper in NSW.**"

A Representative in the Northern Territory Legislative Council had **strong words about Darwin. He was a Rep from Alice Springs**, and wanted the Territory to move its capital to Alice....

He said that Darwin is a "political excrescence" and that "Darwin's only imports were full beer bottles and empty Public Servants, and its only exports were empty beer bottles and full Public Servants." **He presumably thought that Alice Springs would be better.**

In Newcastle suburbs, a man went to a house in Wickham and tried unsuccessfully to talk to his wife. He left the house, walked across the road, and then **fired four shots from a pea-rifle into the house**. He tried to re-enter the house, but was struck with **an 8-pound door stopper** thrown by an upstairs resident. He was taken stunned and concussed to the hospital....

This story interests me because I happen to live next door to the premises involved. **But don't worry about me. The violence now seems to have stopped.**

As usual, the breweries are warning that **bottled beer will be scarce again this Christmas**. Regular customers might get as many as four bottles, but others would get none. They are saying the shortage is because of the lack of bottles, but others are stating that it is because the breweries can sell the bottled product to places like night clubs and company parties at a higher price....

Beer was always scarce, and the pranks and **manoeuvres pulled by publicans and the breweries were legendary**. "To hell with our regular customers."

Good news. The Government has announced that the **per-person butter ration** for the week before Christmas will be increased from **half a pound to a full pound**. This is a bonus that will allow Christmas cakes to be "much richer and more nutritious."

Ovaltine was being pushed heavily as "a glorious summer drink. Served cold, it keeps you fit and full of energy, keeps you young. Deliciously creamy, cool and refreshing, it is supremely nourishing. Full of malt milk and eggs, and fortified with EXTRA Vitamin A, B, and D and calcium and iron. You should drink it every day, and notice the difference...."

Notice that the spiel has not changed all that much over the years. And the models look much the same as now.....

Perhaps they **are** the same people. Maybe that is what they meant when they said "keeps you young."

On Sunday December 18th, **three people drowned in NSW and five in Victoria**....

Comment from 2018. Year after year, such tragedies occur. Also deaths from bush fires. Year after year, we feel bad about them and do nothing. We - collectively and nationally - could. But we don't. Maybe we should.

SONGS OF 1949

All I Want for Christmas is my Two Front Teeth	Spike Jones
Buttons and Bows	Doris Day
Cruising Down the River	Russ Morgan
Ghost Riders in the Sky	Vaughan Monroe
Some Enchanted Evening	Perry Como
You're Breaking My Heart	Vic Damone
Lucky Old Sun	Frankie Laine
Mule Train	Frankie Laine
I Can Dream, Can't I	Andrew Sisters
Rudolf the Red-nosed Reindeer	Gene Autry
Far away Places	Bing Crosby

MOVIES OF 1949

Abbott, Costello meet Killer	Boris Karloff
	Bud and Lou
Adam's Rib	Spencer Tracy
	Kath Hepburn
All the King's Men	Broderick Crawford
I was a Male War Bride	Cary Grant
	Ann Sheridan
The Inspector General	Danny Kaye
Kind Hearts and Coronets	Alec Guinness
My Friend Irma	Diana Lynn, Martin and Lewis
On the Town	Gene Kelly
	Frank Sinatra
The Third Man	Orson Welles
	Joseph Cotton

ELECTION FOREPLAY

The election was due to be held on December 10th. On the Monday before the election, **Mr Jack Lang, of the Lang Labor Party**, made a series of allegations about the financial dealings of Mr Chifley on national radio in his election speech, and then in a series of public meetings for the rest of the week.

Apparently, over the period from 1930 to 1940, Mr and Mrs Chifley had loaned money to certain constituents so that these people could buy their own houses. They had been refused loans by the banks, and turned to the Chifleys for help. There were 24 loans in all. **The sensation was over the interest rates charged.**

Home loans are always provided by the banks at a rate a few percentage points lower than commercial rates. In this case the rates charged by the Chifleys are in between the two, but **closer to the commercial rates**. Mr Chifley had for years railed against the banks, claiming that **they were extorting money from homeowners, and making huge profits as a consequence**. Now it was revealed that he himself had lent money and **at a rate higher than the banks would have charged**. After all the political mileage that Chifley got out of attacking the banks, here he was hoist by his own petard.

Mr Lang's political career went back to the 1920's. He had been Labor Premier of NSW in the 1930's, and at that time had tried to avoid paying interest on Government loans they had arranged with England. Subsequently, he had been forced out of the Labor Party, and he formed his own Party that was not at all friendly to Labor. Now, he flashed into action with a beautifully executed ambush. He had researched the Registrar General's Office in Sydney and found the mortgages, and they had been checked and verified by his solicitors. **There was no doubt that his facts were correct.** He gave the details of each loan in his election speech, and elsewhere, and masterfully laid out all the details for everyone to see.

The effect was significant. Those people who liked Chifley said that he was worthy of commercial rates because it was a commercial proposition. Those who disliked him said he was another capitalist preying on the vulnerable. **But very good mud had been thrown, and some of it stuck.**

Chifley made little defence. He objected to his wife being drawn into politics, and said he had done the humane thing, the rates he charged were lower than any other rate they could have got - if they could have got a loan at all. At an open-air meeting at Lang Park at Bathurst, he let himself go a little. He said that he would refrain from talking about personal affairs of candidates. He added, "There is one matter that I think I should refer to, and that is to a Labor rat in this country. **He is a Labor rat. I am not pursuing any further a Labor rat down the sewer.**" He simply took the approach that his personal matters were his own affair, and once again stood on his record. He hoped people would trust him.

Mr Lang was a trifle less restrained. He proclaimed, "The man who would stand on a platform and advocate reduction of interest, and call lenders blood-sucking usurers, while at the same time practicing usury himself, is a hypocrite, and when I see hypocrisy, I am prepared to expose it." It was the Jack Lang of old, in full flight.

Chifley was undoubtedly the loser here. One consolation for him was that Lang lost his seat, and in a perverse way, it might have been that this way-laying of Chifley had reflected badly on him too.

ELECTION RESULTS

The Labor Government in New Zealand had been kicked out a few weeks ago, and the Attlee Labour Government in England was clearly about to follow. **Could Chifley pull off a stunning reversal, and win despite all the odds stacked up against it?**

The answer is no, he could not. He, and his team, could not even get close. He had won in 1946 with a comfortable majority, but now he was routed. By Sunday the count was 69 for the Coalition and only 43 to Labor. Nine seats were still in doubt, and most of these eventually went to the Coalition. It was a landslide.

Editorials round the nation generally agreed that the causes were quite in line with what **we** have thought as we went through the year. They suggested that various attempts to socialise the nation, and to regiment the population, worked against Labor. Many found fault with **Chifley's obsession with the Depression**, and his apparent belief that the electorate felt the same way. Then again, his "unbelievable decision to not promise reforms, but **to stand on his record**, smacks of arrogance, and ignorance of the electorate." One writer thought he had it right: "Chifley was twenty years behind his times. He still thought that a real politician did not have to sell himself, and that people would **somehow** know that his intentions were noble. Menzies showed him up as an old-fashioned and working class man, who said nothing because he had nothing to say."

But he could not have achieved all of this without some first-rate help. Our friend Arthur Calwell gets a few bouquets here. Every editorial writer slams his administration of the WAP. Doctor Evatt and Eddie Ward, whom we have scarcely reported, got considerable mention as well. It was **these three men who would occupy prime positions in the new Labor Opposition, and it was not until they were all gone that Labor won back control of Parliament**.

CHANGES TO THE GUARD

New Government meant new Members, and strange names were added to the Ministry. Most of these did quite well over time. Do you remember any of them?

Mr McMahon went on to become Prime Minister, and Mr Hasluck became Governor General. Mr Cramer was at one time the Minister for the Army, and Mr Jack became the long-standing Member for North Sydney.

Equally well, in a landslide, there were certain to be Ministers who lost their jobs. One such that I was particularly pleased to see go was a gentleman called John Dedman, who had irritated me – or really my father – when he was the Minister for Tail-less Shirts in the War years. It was doubly pleasing to see his seat won by Hubert Opperman, who had in the twenties been a world champion racing cyclist. Opperman had founded the company that sold Malvern Star bicycles, which many a young person, like myself, rode everywhere in those days. He was a childhood hero of mine, and did a thorough, measured job in his decade in Parliament.

DUGAN AND MEARS

These two gentlemen, **about to become notorious**, were already well known to the prison system. They had been convicted together of assaulting and robbing an elderly woman. They were armed with a gun at the time. **Dugan had escaped three times previously, and Mears once before.** Both were serving a ten-year sentence.

On the day after the election, Mears was brought from Long Bay Gaol to Central Police Court to be charged with possession of a gun in the above assault. Dugan was brought along, and was listed as a witness. While Mears was in the dock, Dugan used a hacksaw to cut through an iron bar strategically placed over a door in his cell. When the Court stopped for lunch, Mears was brought back to the cell, and they then managed to remove the sawn bar, and squeeze through the gap that had been created. They were then able to walk out of the police station, and escape.

The newspapers were full of this daring exploit. Dugan's previous escapes and captures were full of excitement and drama, and now was added the revelation that he had been bragging that he would be out for Christmas. **Police started a major manhunt for the pair.** For example, they swept on the Lidcombe State Hospital, and searched it from cellar to attic, and they raided houses in Surry Hills, Redfern, Alexandria, King's Cross and East Sydney. They also staked out the cabin, on the George's River, where the pair had been captured on the previous occasion.

Questions were being asked. **Where, oh where, would they get a hacksaw? In a cake? Surely not.** And how would they get it from Long Bay to Central? After all, they were handcuffed together, and in eye-catching prison clothing. An inquiry was quickly held, and three warders were suspended and, next day, dismissed.

Meanwhile, the search went on. It was made more difficult because of the number of false tip-offs that were being phoned in by friends of the pair. Dugan wrote two letters to Sydney newspapers. In them he objected to being called a gunman. He claimed that the police were doing that so that they could shoot him on sight. Then, he claimed, they would put the gun beside his body, douse him and the area with gin, and claim he committed suicide. It was a bit lurid.

But there I have to leave this story. It developed into a major event in the New Year, but I am afraid I must save an account of it till then.

CHRISTMAS IN EUROPE.

This is the most normal Christmas in Europe and America since 1938. Goods are said to be plentiful, and foodstuffs are readily available. For example, lighted Christmas trees were to be seen in every city and town. Hams and poultry were so plentiful that the Germans no longer regarded them as luxuries – they were more interested in the latest cars and ingenious toys. The same was true in each of the European nations, and was a sign that some sort of recovery was well under way, and that maybe the hard times of the War and the re-construction were almost gone.

The King sent a message. King George VI had not been well for much of 1949. He had been scheduled to come to Australia for a tour this year, but had been unable to do so. There was talk at one stage that the illness was very serious, but it turned out not to be. Now, he was up and almost running, and saying those platitudinous words that are so welcome, that he has said for a decade. And which, incidentally, his daughter Queen Elizabeth II says with equal aplomb every year.

The King announced: Each year I value more highly the opportunity of this message I am able to give you on Christmas Day. In no other way would it be possible for me to be in such direct personal touch with the many friends to whom I am speaking.

I told you a year ago of the volume of sympathy for me in my illness that had come from every part of the world. Those good wishes, I am thankful to say, have been largely fulfilled so that I am now able again to undertake many public duties which, under doctors' orders, I was for a while obliged to forgo.

More, I would say how touched and encouraged I have been by the affectionate concern of millions in these islands, and far outside them. May this season, and the New Year that follows it, bring you real happiness.

Comment. Corny but welcome.

COMING SOON: REDS UNDER OUR BEDS

Throughout this book, I have mentioned the Reds who were intent on changing our world. Some wanted a violent revolution with blood running in the streets, and other wanted great changes by non-violent processes. I mentioned the set-back that came with the miners' strike, but said it was only temporary.

And that is the point I want to address here. In the future, starting now, **Communism will become a major political concern for the nation.** With the arrival of Bob Menzies at the Lodge, the Reds were pushed further and further into the limelight. In particular, this venerable gentleman decided soon, after his election, that he would hold a referendum that would declare that the Communist Party, and all its affiliates, were illegal bodies, and ban them and all their members from jobs and a full range of entitlements.

He held that referendum, and it was defeated only by a small margin. **But after that, he never let up on the Reds.** And it was always useful to him. Every time that, over the next 16 years, he felt that he was losing popularity, he played the Red Card, and found some way to suggest that the Reds were under our Beds, and that **only he could get them out**.

SUMMING UP 1949

This year, 1949, was undoubtedly one of the most active in the 30 years that this series of books has covered. It was the last year of the half-century and it seemed that a number of things that had been left unfinished were up for the doing. In other years, I often include twenty pages of pure trivia, where I report on matters that have no links really to other stories. But not this year. Almost every piece of trivia is used to show some other side to a story, or to suggest to the reader that there is something going on that I cannot report on, but would like to.

For example, I have included almost nothing on health issues, like TB and polio. A controversy over nurses' pay was worthy of inclusion. Eddie Ward was caught up on the edge of some corruption in New Guinea, and while he was completely blameless, the episode showed a lot about how Government sometimes works. There were only brief mentions of sport in the whole book. I regret that I could not more fully cover these, and other matters.

The event of the year was the coal strike. The miners and all unionists, and the Communists, learned the hard way that pushing strikes too far was pointless, and that in the long run the Government had all the tools necessary to beat any strike that was called.

Then there was the **little spat between McGirr and Warwick Fairfax**. Now, I appreciate Fairfax's position in that he was the editor of a newspaper, and he could put into it anything he wanted. But I find it a bit rich for him to say that he gave equal space to opposing views. For example, his paper printed about 6000 column-inches on the miners' strike in July, and less than 100 inches were supportive of the miners. To then say his papers was always balanced was stretching a point.

Overall, though, there can be no doubt that **1949 was a prosperous year for the economy**. Jobs were so plentiful that we were said to be "over-employed", housing availability was improving, babies were booming, wages were adequate, **and Bob was about to be your uncle.** Hire purchase was just round the corner, so that if you could not afford the washing-machine now, you could get it on the never-never. **It was a magic world that no one had ever dreamed of before the War.**

There were things to keep an eye on. **Internationally, the Communists and rapacious Capitalists were the main problem, each of them being as silly as the other.** But there was every prospect that we could keep our noses clean, and stay out of any conflicts generated.

Internally, it seemed likely that Menzies would lead a conservative, moderate government that should suit this nation's needs at this time. He already had a reputation for solving contentious policy problems by putting the files in the bottom draw and coming back to them six months later. Apart from a few moments of madness, he stuck to that philosophy for about 16 years. So, given this stability, with the economic boom that we were on the edge of, **the forty-niners could go into the following years with a lot of well-founded confidence.**

If you were born in that year, I hope that was exactly what you did.

READERS' COMMENTS

Tom Lynch, Speers Point. Some history writers make the mistake of trying to boost their authority by including graphs and charts all over the place. You on the other hand get a much better effect by saying things like "he made a pile". Or "every one worked hours longer than they should have, and felt like death warmed up at the end of the shift." I have seen other writers waste two pages of statistics painting the same picture as you did in a few words.

Barry Marr, Adelaide You know that I am being facetious when I say that I wish the war had gone on for years longer so that you would have written more books about it.

Edna College, Auburn. A few times I stopped and sobbed as you brought memories of the postman delivering letters, and the dread that ordinary people felt as he neared. How you captured those feelings yet kept your coverage from becoming maudlin or bogged down is a wonder to me.

Betty Kelly, Wagga Wagga. Every time you seem to be getting serious, you throw in a phrase or memory that lightens up the mood. In particular, in the war when you were describing the terrible carnage of Russian troops, you ended with a ten-line description of how aggrieved you felt and ended it with "apart from that, things are pretty good here". For me, it turned the unbearable into the bearable, and I went from feeling morbid and angry back to a normal human being.

Alan Davey, Brisbane. I particularly liked the light-hearted way you described the scenes at the airports as American, and British, high-flying entertainers flew in. I had always seen the crowd behaviour as disgraceful, but your light-hearted description of it made me realise it was in fact harmless and just good fun.

In 1964, HMAS Voyager, an Australian destroyer, was sunk in a collision with the air-craft carrier, Melbourne. Stamp collecting was disappearing as a hobby, wine was no longer plonk, and mothers were waging war on old-fashioned tuck-shops. (God bless them. The tuck-shops, not the mothers). The Beatle cult was angering some people. The Tab: to be on not to be? Can true Reds get fat? Did Billie Graham have lasting effects? Prostitution was proposed as a safety valve against rape. Judy Garland got bad Press in Melbourne and left Oz in a sulk.

In 1967, postcodes were introduced, and you could pay your debts with a new five-dollar note. You could talk-back on radio, about a brand new ABC show called "This Day To-night." Getting a job was easy with unemployment at 1.8 % – better that the 5% 50 years later. Arthur Calwell left at last. Whitlam took his place. Harold Holt drowned, and Menzies wrote his first book in retirement.

****

Born in 1968?
What else happened?
AUSTRALIAN SOCIAL HISTORY

RON WILLIAMS

In 1968, Sydney had its teeth fluoridated, its sobriety tested for alcohol with breathalisers, and its first Kentucky Fried. And it first heart transplant. There was still much opposition to the Vietnam War and demos, often violent, were everywhere all the time. The casino in Tasmania was approved. We won a pot of gold at the Olympics, Lionel Rose became the first Aboriginal to become a World Boxing Champion, and poet Dorothea Mackellar died at the age of 82.

Born in 1970?
What else happened?
AUSTRALIAN SOCIAL HISTORY

RON WILLIAMS

In 1970, President Nixon's war in Vietnam, and now Cambodia, was getting unpopular in the USA and Oz. Melbourne's Westgate Bridge fell into the water and killed 35 workmen. The Queen, Prince Phillip, and two kids came to Oz. They liked it, so the Pope came later. Margaret Court, John Newcombe, Shane Gould, and Raylene Boyle all did well overseas, and made us think we were world-beaters. Mick Jagger starred in "Ned Kelly".

****

Chrissi and birthday books for Mum and Dad and Aunt and Uncle and cousins and family and friends and work and everyone else.

Don't forget a good read and chuckle for yourself.